IDITAROD LEADERSHIP

IDITAROD LEADERSHIP

UNLEASHING THE POWER OF THE TEAM

LEVERAGE THE ADVENTURE TO BECOME A MASTER LEADER

CHRIS FULLER

Iditarod Leadership

For more information on the Iditarod Trail Sled Dog Race®, including becoming a volunteer, please go to http://www.iditarod.com

ISBN 978-1-60743-839-7

Cover Photo: Mush! Richard Legner
http://flickr.com/photos/legrisak/legric@gmail.com

Contents

*"Adventure is critical for the soul.
It's a part of finding who you are."*

Prologue

A Race to Save Lives

January 21, 1925—It had been a frigid winter and like most days the temperature never even reached zero—today, the high would be -5°F.

The usual winter sicknesses made their rounds throughout the town, keeping the doctor busy. However, a new strain—something different—had been attacking their immune systems, and the young Inuits were particularly vulnerable. The process of diagnosing, treating, assessing and altering treatment had led to this point. Dr. Curtis Welch had come to the realization that what he was chasing was a deadly outbreak of Diphtheria.

The villagers of this remote northern port located along the Bering Sea would not survive without the antitoxin. The search begins for the life saving serum, but as time wore on, the distance grew with every telegraph . . .

Finally, the only serum in Alaska was found.

Where? How many miles? His heart sank. A thousand miles away? A thousand miles of frozen, Alaskan wilderness away?

The serum was in the care of Dr. J.B. Beeson at the Alaska Railroad Hospital in Anchorage.

How fast can it be transported? The usual method for transportation during the summer months was steamship, but the sea had iced in the town since October, and it wouldn't thaw until June. What about planes? Would someone be so daring as to fly during these conditions and attempt the landing? The only two available planes had been disassembled and neither had ever flown in winter. The call for help reached the Governor and the request for an alternate route was approved. The Alaskan Railroad ferried the medicine more than 250 miles north to Nenana. But from that point on, the traveling was treacherous.

From there began what became known as "The Great Race of Mercy."

Just before Midnight, January 27, with the clock ticking, the serum and the survival of the town was transferred into the hands of rugged men and their teams of sled dogs who would race across some of the most brutal terrain and the harshest conditions that Mother Nature has to offer.

When the first musher left Nenana, the temperature reportedly hovered at -50°F. The volunteer mushers transferred this "Baton of Life" 18 times—until it reached the hands of Leonhard Seppala and his Lead dog, Togo, considered by many to be the true heroes of the run. Together they covered the most hazardous stretch of the route and carried the serum farther than any other team.

The twentieth and final transfer was made and, according to legend, the serum was nearly lost when a huge gust of wind toppled the sled of this final musher. The musher frantically dug the serum out of the snow with his bare hands, righted his sled and continued on. February 2 at 5:30 a.m., just five days and seven hours after leaving Nenana, the Norwegian, Gunnar Kaasen, and his Lead dog, Balto, arrived on Front Street in Nome.

Salvation came through Courage, Skill, Teamwork, and Perseverance!

Arrival

We've all heard the saying, "If you're not the Lead dog, the view never changes." But I've discovered that the true leader of the team isn't the Lead dog. The ultimate leader is back in the sled. The leader is the one with the vision and execution strategy. This doesn't mean that there aren't times when the leader is up front running with his/her Lead dogs and showing them the way, it simply means that being a great leader is about servant leadership.

The race for which the Iditarod began was first run back in 1925. It was a mission to get life-saving serum from Anchorage to Nome in the dead of the Alaskan winter. It took innovative thinking as well as courageous leaders to forge the path and make history across dangerous terrain.

In 2008, I embarked upon my own Iditarod adventure. It was nearly 4700 miles to get there. Six days of hard travel and 8 cities from the warm Fort Worth winter to the arid Arizona climate to the northwest—a tough but rewarding week of speaking to conference rooms full of executives from a couple of dozen different companies about leadership and growing their personal influence.

From Portland, I flew back through Seattle to Anchorage, all the way to the frozen region of Kotzebue and, finally, to my destination. The exhaustion had turned to exhilaration as I had made it to Nome, Alaska and was in the beginnings of experiencing what I had set out to do.

I had set out to mush a team of dogs—to learn and experience a very small slice of what the Iditarod participants experience. I had walked Front Street, inspected the finish line, and looked out over the frozen Bering Sea. Elated, the next day I rendezvoused with Nils—the musher who would become my teacher/mentor/sensei for the week. His wife, Diana, was remarkable in her own right, and their daughter, Lizzie, pranced around as the princess of her castle! We talked for awhile about this book and spent some great time at their home, walking through the kennel and getting to know his family, human and canine alike. When he asked if I was ready to go for a sled ride, I felt like a kid—being asked by my uncle if I wanted to go for a motorcycle ride—YEAH!

The feelings of being an excited kid quickly changed to feeling like a child when the first order of business was to put me *IN* the sled. With Nils behind, I felt like a 12-year-old that for some reason was having to ride in a child's stroller wrapped in a couple of layers and zipped in—he and Diana both had made sure that I was wearing the proper attire to not bring harm upon myself as a greenhorn to the Alaskan winter wilderness.

I had quoted the statement for years, "If you're not the Lead dog, the view never changes," and now I am here to tell you that the view DOESN'T change—and neither does the SMELL! Being in that sled put me right in the line of both sight and smell—front row center!

One of the minor details that Nils had left out was that the dogs get so excited to run and pull that the excitement soon turns to the need to relieve themselves—just as soon as they start running!

Further, they had been in Anchorage a week or 2 earlier and at race events—if there are any teams that happen to have a bit of sickness, they quickly pass the bug to other teams, and it takes a few weeks and some medication to remedy the effects.

As we took off like a shot out of the kennel area and circled the house before heading out to open trail—the excitement transitioned into their biological needs, and I quickly wondered if maybe I should have purchased a pair of sunglasses that came with windshield wipers and a gas mask! Small price to pay, I guess, for living the dream!

The next trip out, I did get a sled of my own, however, it was tethered to Nils—so I could get the feel of the sled and riding on the runners, without actually being in charge or trusted with a team! After awhile—being the person that I am—I was back behind Nils experimenting with my sled, trying to see how it would react to different weight changes, to different balancing acts, trying to equate it to my experience of wake boarding and tubing behind boats back in Texas. It wasn't—and I soon flipped my sled on a turn and planted face first into the snow as we took the loop to start heading back home!

The rest of the journey back to the house was more tame, as I learned my position and reduced the experimentation back to a remedial level.

The next day I couldn't wait to get back to Nils and the kennel—it would be my first day of mushing—I was actually going to get to run a team, and I was charged with excitement.

The experience was incredible and with minimal trouble (not without experimentation but without much in the way of negative results!).

That leads me to the "rest of the story" . . . after running that team for several trips, Nils asked if I was up for adding another dog. True to my nature, I quickly agreed and said, "Let's go for it!"

I have to admit that I was a little nervous. On my team were not only dogs that had run the Iditarod previously, but also some of Diana's dogs, and I felt the responsibility of keeping the team safe and intact while I learned to mush.

As I breathed in the crisp air and took in the scenery, the line between reality and the surreal was a bit blurry at that moment. I was exactly where I wanted to be, doing exactly what I wanted to do! Watchful of Nils, it seemed like slow motion as he leaned down to pull his snow hook from the ground, and I watched as his team of 14 to 16 dogs started out of the kennel to the path that circumnavigated the house—my cue to release my hook and follow. My mind was racing—this is going to be a more power-ful, more dangerous experience than I had anticipated. Already having done the research, I knew that most of the dogs could pull about 300 pounds each. I had 7 dogs, which equated to 2100 pounds of pull. Even at 185, I anticipated needing to stand on the brake to keep the team in check and in control! As a result, I abandoned the success of starting the previous excur-sions by standing on the drag and planted my weight firmly on the brake. Within 10 seconds, we hit the turn and an area of buried trees that had caused a raised area on the surface. In a blink, the "bump" shifted my weight to the right side of the brake and the right spike bit into the snow. I was thrown off the sled and was upside down being dragged by the team, desper-ately trying to live out rule #1 of mushing—NEVER LET GO OF THE SLED! I begin saying to myself . . . hold on Fuller. What happened? How did I get here? Flip your body back over and maybe the sled will flip with you. Does Nils see me? Dear God, I hope he doesn't have a camera. Wait—the dogs poop on the run. There are a combined 23 dogs running in front of me—dodge the land mines!

Nils did see my predicament. No, he didn't have a camera, and by the time he got my team stopped, I was covered in . . .

Snow—I was covered in snow!

How could I have flipped the sled? Ten seconds into the mis-sion, and I'm on my backside—and in the poo!

The other 21.9 miles we ran that day were pristine, but the start was ugly. I immediately wondered how many leaders have been or are in just that situation: you've been given a team and a mission, and you are in the poo! Upside down and scrambling to get on top of your "sled" before the leaders above you or those around you see what has happened and, Dear God—I hope no one has cameras to capture this!

One of the things we can all learn from the Iditarod is the value of leadership and its impact on the team. Within these pages you'll find lessons that I've learned over the years about creating and leading teams and the dramatic effect a few strategic changes can make in your organization.

To illustrate these leadership concepts, I have combined personal experiences with business fiction that uses stories that will stay with us and embed concepts deeper than simply stating truths. Written as an adventure, the characters are a compilation of multiple people and no one person in particular.

With that in mind . . .

Let the journey unfold.

1

The Journey Begins

*All great adventures start with us deciding
to get ourselves to a place where they can occur.
Great adventures rarely occur back home
in the "La-Z-Boy."*

I stepped off of the helicopter into the Alaskan wilderness. My heart raced with adrenaline and I hoisted my backpack across my shoulder and pushed forward, scanning the landscape. I took a deep breath to soak in my surroundings and calm my mind, and the air smelled clean and heavy with the moisture from the snow. The mundane aspects of my life back home seemed to fade, like a distant memory.

I knew that there would be others joining me for this mushing adventure, but I had no idea who they'd be. Like one of those reality shows on television, *Survivor* or *The Amazing Race*, we'd be thrust together in a small group with an authentic dogsled and a trained musher as our guide. Most, if not all, would choose to leave after a few days. I'd been told that on one previous trip, the entire group went back to their lives, opting out after the first ten hour grueling journey. I was determined not to be one of them. I had come to finish the race.

Through research and a degree of serendipity, I had found my way to this adventure. It was run by a musher named Nils, and over the last few weeks we had corresponded about the details over the phone and via emails. There would be a time of preparation, of learning to control a team and a sled, followed by a three day wilderness adventure. For those unfamiliar with the real deal—it could be termed a mini Iditarod. The winner of the race was a winner in perseverance, character, and strength. Endurance and mental toughness would be just as critical as physical stamina.

A guide met us at the airport in Nome, traveled with us on the helicopter ride down to the base camp and now led us into a small pub named Husky's. It was the kind of place where locals came at the end of a long day to have a beer or coffee and unwind from the day while winding their own stories from past and present adventures. It was a new experience to see a parking lot contain snow machines and sleds as well as trucks and cars.

It was a simple place, no frills, with framed newspaper articles lining the walls. About half-way towards the bar, an article written in a local newspaper caught my eye. I dropped my backpack and moved closer to read what it said.

March 2006—The 49 year old, Kasilof Musher, Paul Gebhardt (Bib #84), left the Kripple checkpoint and got disoriented. He thought he missed the trail and doubled back; even passed a fellow rider and went back to the checkpoint only to figure out he was on the right trail all along. That mistake cost him six hours.

I read the rest of the article in disbelief. As an experienced musher, Paul knew that no matter what mistakes a musher made, the dogs had to pay for it. His dogs ran six hours more because of his mistake. He was upset with himself and had a hard time shaking it. Finally, he stopped himself and realized his bad attitude about his mistake was going to transmit to the team and their effectiveness going forward. He didn't want the team carrying that attitude and knowing he set the tone, he chose to change himself.

He was able to gather his composure, fight through a number of additional harrowing experiences and surge forward, ultimately, to reach the Burled Arch of Nome and claim his third top-ten finish. The lost musher made a comeback!

I stepped back and sat down at the bar, wondering about how many times my team had paid the price for mistakes I made as a leader. I, myself, had had some great bosses and some who were tragic examples of leadership—and boy did we pay!

Every Example of Leadership (Great or Tragic) has taught me something— what to do or what NOT to do

My thoughts retreated to the time I was under a leader whose perspective of his people was that they were "dogs," beasts of the field meant to bring in the harvest for him. He seemed blind to the need to care for the team and to know where each team member was—who was on the fringe of burning out, who needed encouragement, and who was in desperate need of more training runs. The trail of carnage in the wake of poor leadership was astounding. And then my mind wandered to another leader, Jim, whose manner of leading, connectedness and encouragement made me want to give more and inspired me to be the best I could. It is in my nature to give my all, but how I felt at the time and how I feel today about those portions of my life is a stark reminder of the difference the right-minded leader can make on their team.

The Trail we carve as Leaders profoundly affects the next generation

A man lowered himself onto the barstool beside me.

"Evening, Charlie," the bartender said, addressing him. "How was the trail today?" He pulled a pilsner glass out of the freezer bin and grabbed the wooden tap, pouring a perfect Ale. The man beside me shook off the cold, and draped his coat over the back of the chair. He appeared to be in his early 50s, but I couldn't tell if his balding made him appear older.

"I'm living every man's dream," he replied to the bartender's question. "To be on a great adventure and come back and hang out in the pub! It just doesn't get any better than this, does it?"

I smiled and lifted my cup at the strangers.

The adrenaline I felt when I stepped off of the helicopter hadn't ceased. I sensed that I was about to embark upon the greatest adventure of my life, but my head was swimming. I thought about my family. I knew I would miss them this week. I thought about my team back home. I had been promoted to VP last year after having been the top-rated consultant for eight months in a row. All of a sudden, I went from being responsible for just myself to having a team depending on me to lead them toward success. And we had been successful, relatively. But there was a lot more to learn. What could I do differently? What did my team think of my leadership? I know I'm a top producer, that's what earned me the promotion, but am I a good leader? Were they better off now than before I was in charge? How many times had they paid the price for my mistakes? How will my colleague lead them differently while I spend the week away? Getting things done was my strength and my pride. Getting things done with a team is a different set of competencies altogether.

I knew that this trip would be critical for my growth. Our leadership perspectives are developed through the examples of those that have led us, and the trail we carve profoundly affects the next generation of leaders. In my work to coach executives and CEOs, it dawned on me that, like the competitors in the Iditarod, there were several types of employees and team members. Maximizing their skills and talents was critical to the success of the team. I had been fascinated with the link between the great race and leadership since the day I read about the Iditarod back in the early 2000s after seeing the end of the annual race on TV.

I started envisioning the positions of team members within an organization in the same way the mushers categorize their dogs. As a part of the makeup of an Iditarod team, there are four distinct positions the dogs fill (Lead dogs, Swing dogs, Team dogs, and Wheel dogs), and each has its distinct characteristics and purpose. Any position not filled or not filled correctly will weaken the team, and it will have to work harder to finish the race, if it can finish at all. My studies had led me to know these things in theory, but I'm the type of person that needs to experience things to make the connection and correlation authentic.

The pub continued to fill up with what I thought might be other Iditarod adventure seekers. I was just about to introduce myself to one small group when the room erupted.

I hadn't met Nils in person and was surprised at the response of the people as he came in. Was he a legend around these parts or just a great guy? An expert musher, he has been through and seen it all.

When he walked through the door the pub buzzed with anticipation and excitement. He immediately addressed the group. "If you're not dedicated, pack up now and save face," he said. "Save yourself the time and effort. If you didn't come here to ride eight hours facing down the wind and the snow, move on."

The room erupted once again. I looked around nervously and saw a few other nervous faces, too. "If you thought this would be a fun, easy vacation, this isn't for you," Nils warned. "You won't last out there and you could kill your team, your fellow mushers, or your guide."

Little did we know that in the next few days almost everyone in that pub would be heading home, deeming the race too difficult to finish.

**Victories are easily won
on paper in the lodge.
The proof lies outside the lodge on trail—
where plans meet reality**

"The real Iditarod race is a marathon, not a sprint. For Iditarod Mushers, the facts are this: you are in a grueling race. You and your team of 12 to 16 dogs must cover over 1100 miles of the roughest terrain Mother Nature has to offer. Your marathon stretches into a couple of weeks, not hours. If you are going to make it to the end—if you are going to finish the race—then you need to pace yourselves and your team. We have to take the mindset that we are in it for the long haul. Leaders with a short-term perspective will abuse their team for short-term results, only to learn their team is exhausted and can't go on. If a dog goes down, you can take the dog out of the race, but you cannot replace any of your team!"

Nils continued, "Team Sport. This race is a *team* sport. If anyone attempted this same course without a team it would take months to complete, if you could even make it at all. By the time you crossed the finish line, the fans would have gone home, and the banners would be frayed by the arctic winds!"

At that moment I thought about one of the top reasons why small businesses and even teams within large organizations fail. It's that the owner or project leader is doing everything on their own. They are the secretary, the accountant, the salesperson, the production manager, the purchasing department. And most often, they are in the lead position at the front of the pack, dragging the team along behind them.

Leading a team is a different skill set than accomplishing great individual feats

Nils had not stopped his introductory speech, "This adventure will only give you a taste of what goes on out in the Alaskan wilds. If you complete this course, you will be among a select few.

"In the morning, we'll start where all great mushers start— in the kennel—if you can't take the smell or the hard work, or if you're not a dog person, the kennel will weed you out. Be outside at 7:00 a.m."

He turned and walked out.

The crowd scattered, some going for a drink at the bar and others huddling at small tables. A group of people left for the bunkhouse, and I saw one person packing it in out of the corner of my eye. Are some quitting even before they begin?

Back at the bunkhouse, the surroundings were rough. Definitely not a four-star hotel. Empty bunks were lined up around the walls; the floors were bare with an occasional small rug near each bunk. The walls contained a number of wilderness photographs. A closer look revealed the photographer was Diana, Nils' wife. A wood burning stove in the corner heated up the entire room.

I placed my gear on my bunk, and one person in particular caught my attention. He was the oldest one in the group by at

23

least a few years, and he wore a tweed cap and a long coat that looked as if it might be cashmere.

"Hi," I said, extending my hand.

The man nodded and forced a smile. He removed a black leather glove and shook my hand.

"Man, this is great. You ready for this? Should be all kinds of incredible experiences out here."

"Yeah, incredible," the man said, rolling his eyes.

He turned and placed his backpack on the bunk, opening it. Inside everything was organized, fitting perfectly into the bag, with a series of sub-compartment organizers for each category of clothing. I couldn't tell if someone packed this for him or if he was that good as he had pulled it from a box that had obviously been shipped ahead. I started to ask about it when the lights began to blink, a sign they would soon be off.

I'll have to wait until tomorrow to get my answer as the lights flicker again and are suddenly turned out.

Still running on adrenaline, I toss and turn for what seems like an hour. Not wanting to disturb the others I pulled out a small book lamp, clipped it on the bill of my cap and pointed the light toward a small writing journal I'd bought at the airport. Reflecting on the day and trying to empty my mind, I jotted down some thoughts before finally nodding off to sleep.

Tomorrow is the start of a great adventure.

Checkpoints

All great adventures start with us deciding to get ourselves to a place where they can occur. Great adventures rarely occur back home in the "La-Z-Boy."

Every Example of Leadership (Great or Tragic) has taught me something—what to do or what NOT to do.

The Trail we carve as Leaders profoundly affects the next generation.

Victories are easily won on paper in the lodge. The proof lies outside the lodge on the trail— where plans meet reality.

Business and life are marathons, just like the Iditarod. We have to strategically pace ourselves in order to achieve success.

Leading a team is a different skill set than accomplishing great individual feats.

Leaders and Mushers who are satisfied with the status quo will rarely leave the comfort of the Lodge.

Iditarod

The word "Iditarod" has several attributed meanings yet two specifically apply to leadership. One meaning is "distance or distant place" and the other is said to mean "clear water." Could there be a better tie-in to discuss the end game of leadership? I need to achieve my goal, I have a distance to go, and in order to get there, I will need as much clarity as I can get my hands on to reach the finish.

Reflections

Where am I in my own journey? Am I still cautiously optimistic about what I could achieve in my own race in life and business? Or am I disoriented and overwhelmed with my direction, desperately panicked to get the team back on track—before the mission gets too far gone?

As a leader, do I make good decisions?
Is my team paying the price for my mistakes?

Think about the challenges stacked against me.
Is there anything that seems insurmountable?
If so, what are they? What would make me leave the race before it has even begun?

2

Self-Awareness

*Your team should be a reflection
of your energy style.*

ike a child on Christmas morning, I woke eager to get the show on the road. I made my way to the kitchen and was surprised to catch Nils alone in the mess hall having a cup of coffee. The kitchen was what you might expect to see in a lodge or camp—metal prep tables, open vats, gas cooktops. I was surprised at the size. You could tell the staff could produce enough food to feed a large group. Facility kitchens all have a similar feel, especially when they're shut down for the night, and a familiar smell of used grease and muted bleach. A couple of the staff was just starting to get things stirring, so I asked if there was coffee on.

"Sure," one of the men said, handing me a Styrofoam cup.

I found my way back to Nils in the mess hall and sat down. We made small talk for a while but he seemed distracted, surveying the yard.

"What's wrong?" I asked.

"I don't like my dogs to bark for no reason. When they bark, I want to know why, and depending on the situation, I will either address the situation or the dog.

"I don't want a kennel full of dogs that are barking all the time. It puts additional stress on the dogs, and I want everyone in the yard to be at peace. I want a *peaceful* kennel."

Now my interest was piqued. My belief was that all dogs barked and that most dogs barked all the time—at anything or nothing. Nils wanted to have an entire kennel full of dogs and not have them bark unless something was wrong?

Beliefs determine behavior

Over the next few days I'd discover that a good number of mushers feel the same way. Some remarked at the quiet strength and power in the Norwegian teams. The dogs are not allowed to jump around and go crazy. They want the dogs focused and not expending any additional energy, prior to them starting a race or leaving a checkpoint.

I reached into my coat and pulled out the small writing journal to make notes.

"Except Lance Mackey," he said.

"What?" I jolted back into the conversation.

"Except Lance Mackey." Nils repeated. "You know the guy that won the last three years' Iditarod."

"Why is that?"

"Lance's dogs go crazy. They jump around, they bark, they yank at the gang line, they even chew through the ropes, I've heard. They, basically, go crazy."

"Really?"

"Take a walk with me."

Self-awareness helps in building the right team for you

We threw on some parkas from the mud room, and I followed him down a narrow path that led to the kennel. It was surrounded by waist-high snow, and although the path was packed, Nils remarked that it was still several meters deep even under our feet. As the cold morning air hit my face, it felt as if I had the beginnings of an instant ice cream headache.

The kennel was small and unremarkable. There were a series of simple wooden-box doghouses in a collective area; straw inside each for warmth . . . and just add snow. That was the kennel in its entirety.

It was Dizzy, a small dog, who was making all the racket. His ears were back, his tail down. Dizzy was focused on the horizon.

"Come on, girl, it's only a caribou. They're out here all the time. Stop fussing about it."

I looked hard at the landscape and saw nothing. "Where do you see that?"

He described where it was, and I still couldn't see it. It reminded me of seasoned business leaders that see things that novices may never see, partly because they don't know what to anticipate or expect.

The clouds moved fast across the sky, and my mind wandered back to Nils' description of Lance's dogs. I wondered what it was like this morning in Lance's kennel. I visualized 7:00 a.m. Metallica and Lance feeding off the energy of his dogs, who would all be a reflection of him. He'd get pumped up, his dogs would sense his energy, and it becomes a cycle. Just like in business, the entire team cranks off of the expressed energy.

In contrast, I could almost hear the quiet serene sounds of a gentle orchestra playing in the background. I thought about the number of startups that I've done and the number of business situations I've been in and how I've used both types of teams within the organizations. Most of the startups or expansions need a tremendous amount of energy. Having team members like Lance's dogs is great—and the energy that everyone feeds off of—with a new venture. As the business unit matures, those same dogs have to either be directed into a new path or at least be monitored for engagement and satisfaction in the more steady daily operations. Energy is crucial to an organization!

I had studied the Iditarod for years, intrigued by the great challenges of the race. But now I was amazed at the ability of certain mushers to raise a team that would reflect them and their desire for peace and controlled energy.

I was equally amazed at Lance's self-awareness. As a student and teacher of leadership, I've both studied and taught about the relationship between a leader's self-awareness, determination and their success. I wondered if this could be an even deeper level of self-awareness for leaders. I wondered about the leaders I coached. I envisioned myself asking them, *Are you self-aware enough to keep from immediately jumping to the Norwegian methodology and say, I need crazy dogs!?* I need dogs that yell and scream and pump me up!

"I suppose the kennel is no different than your business," Nils said. "As we start developing any kennel, the first question must be, what do you want your kennel to feel like?"

What do you want your kennel or team to feel like?

Nils was right. I watched him take care of the dogs, right-ing their bowls, dishing out food to each dog, and watched his interaction with each. Some wanted personal attention, talking to some, petting others. Some just wanted to eat and be left alone. Yet others were just now getting out of their kennels. By this time, it was almost 7:00 a.m. and the other adventurers were milling around.

"Let's get this started," Nils said.

We walked back through the narrow path, stripped off our layers in the mud room, and met up with the others in the mess hall.

Nils came in and addressed the group, moving quickly through the events and processes of the day. He divided us up, and soon we were off on our adventure. For our first tandem training run I was teamed with Joe, an actual Iditarod com-petitor. Joe was a local with weathered skin from the winters outdoors.

"What are you going to wear for sunglasses?" Joe asked. "Did you bring some or do you have goggles? You need a good pair so you can see the trail clearly."

"These are expensive sunglasses." I replied.

Joe took them off my face and examined them. "You'll need more than that," he said.

"Really?"

"If you want to see," he said, laughing.

"I should have brought my ski goggles, or at least my yellow hunting glasses. With the snow blowing as it is—they would be better than my darker glasses."

"No. Not today. The clouds will burn off shortly, and the other lenses would blind you on the trail. Everything would be glaring at you, and you would not be seeing right.

"You can borrow some of mine," Joe said, pulling a pair of blue lenses from his pocket. "I brought a second pair just in case."

Our "lenses" make all the difference in how we see the trail

As we got ready to leave I jumped to the correlation that we teach executives all over the planet. The "Sunglass" principle has a profound impact on each of our lives. The fact is that none of us sees reality. All that we see is OUR reality—all of us see life through our own "sunglasses" and through those lenses the world is "bent" to become our world—our perception. We all have sunglasses, and they almost never leave our eyes.

The first trip out was tethered so we could get the feel of the sled and riding on the runners—without actually being in charge or trusted with a team! After a while, being the person that I am, I was back behind Joe experimenting with my sled—trying to see how it would react to different weight changes—to different balancing acts—trying to equate it to my experience of wake boarding and tubing behind boats back in Texas. I soon flipped my sled on a turn and planted face first into the snow!

The first trip out or project led should be a tandem run to ease the young leaders into their positions on the "sled"

Joe looked back and allowed the dogs to run another 30 to 40 yards before he stopped. I wiped off the snow, embarrassed and wondering if the rest of the trip was going to be so humiliating.

The journey back was easier, as I learned my position and reduced the level of experimentation. After breaking down the gear and returning the dogs to the kennel, I went back into the cabin and removed my boots, gloves and scarf. In my haste, I had missed a small chunk of ice on my cheek which had stayed there since flipping the sled that morning, leaving behind a small line of frostbite. I changed clothes and hung my sweaty, wet gear up to dry along with the others. The bunkhouse now smelled more like a locker room than a ski lodge.

Hearing others in the room describing their day, this may have been the first athletic event for them in years. They were worn out. Their legs were sore from standing all day on the sled. Some had blisters on their feet because their guides were not as helpful in getting them prepared for the ride by not advising them of the appropriate gear to use. And even a few just hated the cold.

Others, like me, were energized and couldn't wait to get back to Nils and the kennel—it would be our first day of mushing. We were actually going to get to run a team and I was charged with excitement.

I was *surprised* to hear that some hated the cold and that another adventurer actually quit. He thought the preparation he had made through Colorado ski trips and winter hunting trip would be sufficient—they weren't! The average temperature in the Alaskan wilderness during the Iditarod season usually ranges from a low of -50°F to a high of +10°F; conditions that neither skiing nor hunting can prepare you for—this was a whole new level. I was thankful that Nils took the time to ask about the boots that I was bringing and to be plain spoken enough to let me know they wouldn't cut it up here. He had sent me the exact model number of the boots to purchase. I wondered if the others just didn't heed the warning.

Preparation is a key to success

Around the fireside that night, Jim, a hand who had lived and worked there for ten years, stoked the embers. The warmth from the fire was mesmerizing and a welcome change from the below zero temperatures endured for the previous 7 hours. On any adventure trip, the fireside is one of the best parts of the day. There is no pressure to perform, just a sense of camaraderie. I was looking forward to hearing the stories of my fellow adventurers.

The group was discussing Sonny's departure from the adventure. "There's an old saying that I know is true." Jim said. "I know it's true 'cause I've seen it all along the trail: If you believe you're gonna succeed or if you believe you're gonna fail—you're probably right."

As we all discussed our experiences, I was somewhat surprised about the diversity of the group. From VPs of Fortune 500 companies to solo-preneurs, from 20-somethings to salty dogs, from warm climates like myself to people well adjusted to the cold and all from different points on the North American map. Some were there because they were adventurous by nature and others because they just needed to break their current cycle. A couple in particular caught my interest.

Jason was a 20-something salesperson from the San Diego area. He had won a sales contest and part of the prize was his participation in this adventure. He was tall, athletic, with an optimistic attitude about life and the mark he was destined to leave on the planet. Listening to him tell his story about the day brought energy into the room. The vigor and refreshing youthfulness reminded me of myself and one of my good friends at the time, Greg, when we were in the same company in our 20s. All of us were competing for Top Dog in sales, and the energy and sparring between us was exhilarating and inspiring. Jason reminded me of those days.

On the other end of the spectrum was Gary. He was the older gentleman I had had a brief encounter with the night before in the bunkhouse. I guessed he was in his mid-50s, although he looked more weathered, and was a corporate executive from Chicago. His additions to the conversation were more grounded in the realities of a life that has *seen* and done a lot more than the rest of us. At times I detected a degree of cynicism in his voice and expressions that made me wonder what brought him there and what his story was.

I went back to my bunk and wrote in my journal for about an hour on new beginnings and the events of the day.

Checkpoints

Self-awareness helps in building the right team for you.

Your Team should be a reflection of your energy style.

Our 'lenses' make all the difference in how we see the trail.

The first trip out or project led should be a tandem run to ease the young leaders into their positions on the "sled."

Reflections

Beliefs drive behaviors. Nils' belief about dogs barking was different from mine—and from the same event—would I have responded differently? It's my kennel. What do I want my kennel to feel like?

My "Sunglasses" or beliefs have been shaped by my personal experiences. Am I aware that I bend reality through my personal "lenses"?

Different projects or ventures may take building teams that match the energy and creativity of the situation. When did my team not match up to a particular task? What would have made it better?

Preparation is a key to success. A component of preparation is getting guidance from the right sources—from those that have tremendous experience at your destination. Who are leaders that I admire that I can learn from on my journey?

3

Communication, Awareness and Skill

*Key elements to succeeding
in your role as leader of a team are:
Communication, Awareness (self and others),
and Constantly Improving Your Skills.*

The group met, again, at 7:00 a.m. sharp in what I would describe as a kind of "tack room" to prepare for today's run.

In the front of the room was a sled with the ropes that the dogs would be attached to during the run. My expectation to immediately start mushing this morning was met with additional training instead. It took me a minute to relax and take it in, when what I really wanted to do was to jump on a sled and go!

As I looked out the window, I took in the scenery: the beautiful landscape—the blanket of white and the distant hills. The stirring of workers opening and closing the tack room doors made me keenly aware of the contrast in smells between the clean Alaskan air and the smell coming from the kennel. Catching a glimpse through the doors, I could see some dogs were standing on their houses, some were rolling in the snow, and all seemed to be anticipating running.

Nils talked first about the need to know the dogs and not just use them—how to connect with the dogs and how the dogs feed off of the musher's energy. If you have a burned-out, angry, or aggressive musher, the dog can feel the anger and aggressive energy.

Jason, the young sales gun from the fireside, asked what most of us were thinking. "Are we going to be in here long? I want to be out in the middle of the adventure! Not in training. I need the wind in my face. I need the crack of the whip."

As Nils was laughing, Jason asked, "What's so funny?"

"Jason, we don't use whips anymore. Whips have been outlawed in the Iditarod for years."

Jason had a confused look on his face. "Really?" He said.

"Yep." Nils picked back up, "If you whip your dogs and they lie down under you, they're not going anywhere and neither are you. Everyone loses."

I thought about the business world and the old school era of command and control leaders. I could see the faces of executives that I've worked with that only had the "hammer" in their leadership tool box and, as a result, treated everything and everyone as if they were a nail—to be beaten down. I thought about the process we took them through, as we worked with them to see and implement other motivational styles to improve employee morale and productivity, such as relationship development, win-win thinking, mentorship and, above all, communication improvement.

Nils returned to his clipboard and said, "What we are about to entrust to you is a valuable set of our team members. It is our job to make sure that you can not only race with your team but that you can care for and operate your team safely. Our livelihood is based on it, and they depend on you as the ultimate leader of the team. This is just some very basic training to keep you and them alive and to have an enjoyable experience. Hopefully, our training throughout the week will equip you to go beyond and be effective as their leader."

Nils continued, "As for real Iditarod competitors and how they train, well, let's just say, 'Amateurs train until they get it right. Professionals train until they can't get it wrong.'"

Amateurs practice until they get it right
Professionals practice until
they can't get it wrong

"If you're out in the wilderness," Nils said, "there are some key elements to not only finishing the race, but to surviving with you and your team intact. Those elements start with communication and awareness and ultimately to developing and refining the skill.

"As I said before in answering Jason's question, there are no whips and there are no reins. In this sport you must be able to communicate effectively to elicit the right response from your team. This sport is no different than any other sport, or team, or culture for that matter. We have our specific 'Language,' and we need to teach you the language of mushing. It may seem remedial to you, but we need to know that you know the dogs' language and what specific words to use to generate a specific response, so no one gets into trouble. Not that it would be the first time someone's mouth has led them off a cliff, but we prefer that not happen while mushing!

"We've created these labels to go around your gloves. The word 'Gee' strap onto your right hand and the word 'Haw' onto your left hand. Use some memory technique to etch these into your brain. Out here we use them every day, so it doesn't take long to memorize them. You have them on your glove, so that will help—or John has made up a cute little saying of GEE you're Right, and HAW, HAW you got left. Now, the word is actually pronounced Ghee, not Jee—but for the most part that may help.

"Guys, it's really simple. There are only a handful of words you need to know. Too many words can equal a confused team, so we keep it simple." Nils moved toward the sled. Grabbing the rope, he said, "When you are lining up your dogs, the phrase 'line out' tells them to keep the team straight and the line tight. 'Hold up' or 'stay still' keeps them in place as well. To get the team going, I use 'mush' or 'hike.' If I want them to go faster, I will usually do a 'kissing sound' or tell them 'pick it up.' To slow or stop the team, 'whoa' is the only word I use."

Nils went on for another half hour or so on communication and dog placement on the rope, which he taught us was the gang line. I fought to pay attention. Mentally, I was anxious and wandering and wondering what effective business boot camp I could create around successful communication and the need for it to be simple, clear and direct. This is so paramount for effective leadership, even more so in challenging times or when an organization needs change.

> ### You don't have to flood your team with words to get them to action
> ### Be clear—Be concise—Be direct

"AWARENESS."

Joe, my guide from yesterday, stepped in to teach this topic. He said the word with such force that it snapped everyone's attention back into focus. "On the trail, you must be aware—aware of your surroundings, aware of yourself, and you must be aware and in tune with each member on your team."

One of the men in the group, Mark, quickly raised his hand. I remember from the fireside stories that his first day didn't go so well. He appeared to be apprehensive about the day and running the sled on his own. After a barrage of questions, seemingly to dispel all the "what ifs," he landed on, "But what about when conditions get bad? Do we turn back?"

"The surroundings dictate your decision-making," Joe answered. "We make decisions out there just like in the real world.

"Regardless of the conditions, you need to know where your own head is at . . . if you're tired or angry or just 'off,' the dogs can tell. Sometimes it affects them; sometimes they'll just keep running and help pull you out of your funk. In any case, you don't want to be the one member of the team that brings down the whole."

Seeming to hone in and address this adventurer in particular, Joe said, "Your nervousness and apprehension is going to translate to the team if you don't grab a hold of it. Dogs can sense fear, and it will affect how they run for you. You will be amazed at how intuitive they are, and they just need to know someone is in charge of the sled."

Getting back on topic, Joe continued, "Awareness of your team. If you listen to your dogs—if you key into them, they will communicate volumes to you. Who is having a bad day? Are they nervous? Is there something ahead in the trail that has them spooked? Do they smell wolves or other wild animals? The only way that you are going to know any of this—is to know your dogs, to know your team. If you have Dizzy on your team—you need to know that she always seems a little nervous—so you may not key off that. However, if Jade seems nervous or not right, it's a problem—she is usually rock steady. Remember, in this situation as a new leader, your team has more experience than you do out on this trail. Leverage that knowledge."

43

Joe turned the training back to Nils for the last portion about skill and knowledge of mushing. I stood there wishing I could push the pause button and write about the correlations to business. I must have been lost in thought because a fellow musher named Rob popped me in the shoulder, as if to say wake up and pay attention.

"There is no substitute for skill of your trade and for many Iditarod mushers—make no mistake—this is their trade, and they are serious about honing their skill. Many of you may know Jeff King, a four-time Iditarod winner. At a book signing for Jeff King, someone asked the question, 'What do you see on the trail that is different from what a rookie or lesser experienced musher might see? His response was, EVERYTHING! He said, 'There is not much that we would see with the same perception. I've seen that piece of the trail so many times that I know, instinctively now, things that have been embedded by years of experience.' So as you're mushing over the next few days, pay attention to your guide—or what we're also calling your mentor. His insight can make all the difference in you making it out there."

Seasoned business leaders see things that novices or the less attentive may never see

Nils changed his stance and seemed to really get down to business now. "Let's make sure everyone is on the same page about the dogs and the sled. Let me give you a quick overview that we will unpack more as we get further into the week.

"You may or may not know that there are 16 dogs on the team for the Iditarod. There are four sets of positions or roles that the dogs fit into. Lead, Swing, Team, and Wheel."

Nils' momentum was broken when Rob, a fellow adventurer, interrupted, "Why 16 dogs?"

"Because," Nils said, "you can't compete with one dog. You can't even compete with two.

"I suppose, if you're just going to buy bread at the grocery store, one dog will do ya, but when you run the Iditarod you are up against teams of 16 trained canine athletes. You have to have enough dogs to have any shot at top 10. What do you guys think we get with 16 dogs that we don't get with 1 or 2?"

Everyone shouted out their answers of speed, stamina, power, sustainable drive, and a handful of other suggestions, some meant to be more humorous than serious.

"So, why not have 30?" Another guy spoke up . . . "or 50?"

Joe stepped up, "I'm sure guys have attempted it. It's sort of the nature of man, right? I'm sure the first dogsled race in history was the day the second sled was made, right?"

Laugher erupted for a brief moment, and Joe continued.

"You can't have two guys and two sleds without one or both of them wanting to race and it just gets bigger and crazier from there. People are going to experiment with exactly how many they can control. In the race, itself, we have to ship food and supplies to each checkpoint to take care of the animals. No one else can help us feed and water the dogs. Do you feel like you could take care of 30 to 50 dogs at each of the 26 checkpoints? Race officials have set the rules at 12 to 16 dogs and it's probably been figured out that is about the maximum to control and care for by one person."

Nils picked back up, "So let's talk about the team and the role of each position.

"The team is, generally, broken up into pairs—and each set / pair has a different role/function. In the front, leading the way, are the Lead dogs, followed by the Swing dogs, Team dogs, and lastly the Wheel dogs."

Nils seemed to stop midsentence and then said, "All right!— enough lecturing for the day—I can see that we're losing you guys, besides, no one came here to hear about mushing—you came to do it, right?"

A resounding "Right" echoed back from everyone.

"Take a quick break and when you come back, get with your mushing guide—they will walk through the process with you and pick your teams."

As Joe and I walked down to the kennel, the sounds were deafening, multiple teams of dogs barking with anticipation to run. The sleds were getting lined out, the gang lines stretching in front and the neck and tug lines extending off. I looked to see if Nils was attempting to quiet the dogs. He wasn't, so I had to assume this was usual for their behavior.

"Set the hook," Joe said. I reached over and grabbed the hook off of the sled handle and placed it in the snow, pressing it the rest of the way with my foot to make sure the fangs of the hook bit into the snow, sufficient to hold the dogs, while we finished harnessing and building the team.

Each dog was so excited as they were loosed from their house in the kennel that they went flying past the other dogs, not yet freed, as if to say, "I'm racing!" The mushing guides knowing each of the team members by name, called them to their position. The teams and the excitement build.

"For the first set of runs, you'll only have 6 dogs. Let's control this team before we trust you with more. Remember, the number one rule of mushing, 'never let go of the sled.' These dogs are trained to run, and whether you are on the sled or not—they will run and leave you lying face down in the snow." Joe smirked at the insinuation of my experience from day one. "Every year we have a musher that dumps their team, and the guides have to try to chase 'em down. Don't let go of the sled!"

**It's your sled and your team—
"Don't let go of the sled!"**

With that—we were off, one by one the teams leaving the yard and heading out to the trail.

We drew the third position so we watched as Rob, Mark and their mentors took off. Each start was a little precarious, and my competitive nature was already kicking in as I sized up my fellow adventurers! What a rush! Heart pounding in the chest—adrenaline coursing through the legs, I felt like screaming, "I'm doing it—I'm mushing!"

Over the next few hours, we ran for about 25 miles, wagon-trailing our teams through the Alaskan countryside. The terrain was more of rolling meadows and a stream than what I imagined the intense wilderness conditions are of the Iditarod Trail.

Just to test Nils' teaching on communication, I decided to throw out other words to the team to see if they would respond. Running through my gambit of Spanish, French and Texas slang, I was somewhat surprised that they all failed to elicit *any* additional action or response from the team. My attempt at additional communication either meant nothing to the team or they simply dismissed it as the ramblings of a rookie leader.

Proving that Nils does know his stuff, making the kissing sounds to the team was pretty effective. It was exhilarating to feel my team respond and pick up the pace. I was really enjoying the journey, and whether they felt it or not, I felt like I was bonding to my new team.

Communicate in *their* language, not *yours*

The dynamics were interesting. I found myself so focused on the trail at times that I barely noticed the countryside. I spent the rest of the trip back moving from being so focused in on keeping up and not making mistakes to taking a deep breath, looking up and taking in the breathtaking beauty of the Alaskan frontier.

Back at the kennel, we spent the better part of an hour breaking down the sled, letting the dogs loose, and feeding and caring for them. It felt right to care for the team and make sure their needs were met before resting myself. There would be plenty of time for food and drink later.

We were all pretty tired from the day. Nils and the crew gave us an hour and a half to clean up before dinner and debrief.

Waiting for my turn at the shower, I grabbed my journal, plopped down on my bunk and pulled out my pen.

Checkpoints

Amateurs practice until they get it right.
Professionals practice until they can't get it wrong.

Seasoned business leaders see things that novices
or the less attentive may never see.

You don't have to flood your team with words to
get them to action. Be clear. Be concise.
Be direct.

It's your sled and your team—"Don't let go of the
sled!"

My team is more intuitive than I think. Be
intentional about what they're picking up
or sensing from me.

Communicate in <u>their</u> language, not <u>mine.</u>

Reflections

Great leaders take time to get to know their team, really know them. How well do I know each individual on my team?

Am I a professional? What do I need to do different to become one?

A team of one or two may be good enough for small ventures but great endeavors can only be achieved with great teams. Am I paying enough attention to the whole team?

4

Knowing Your Dogs

How well your team performs is in direct proportion to how well you know your dogs and put them in the right spot on the team.

fter dinner, we all convened once again fireside. The feeling in the room was that we were tired, but satisfied, and I could feel a sense of pride around the fire. There was a physical, muscular ache, but an emotional satisfaction that we had made it through the day. We were not just talking about an adventure, today we lived a piece of the dream.

John, the guy who created the GEE and HAW bands for the gloves, opened the conversation by saying, "Tomorrow is going to be our first long day. Nils will be here in a minute to work through the logistics and assignments. We want to get an early start on the day, so we will get the talking out of the way tonight. While we're waiting, I wanted to find out more about your experience today. What did you learn about your team today? What did you learn about yourself?"

The stories ran the gambit from bravado about perfect days to laughter and self-ridicule about flipping the sled and chasing down dogs.

As the responses were dying down, John changed gears and turned to me, "Chris, you asked for some more detail around the position of the dogs and the roles they play. I know some of you have mushed before, like Dave and Hans, so you are probably familiar with this, but for the rest of you, I thought I'd take some time to walk you through the anatomy of the team while we're waiting on Nils.

"We have referenced several times the positions of the dogs being Lead, Swing, Team and Wheel. If you ran 2 in each position, that would be 8 dogs. Today you only ran 6. That's what we thought you could handle. As a result, we used dogs that were multi-purpose players. Some teams had dogs that are comfortable running Lead/Swing, and the fact is we swap out those positions at times while racing to give the lead a break, if they need it. For some of the other teams we let the Wheel dogs double up as Team dogs."

"Jim, today we ran Lucky on your team as Wheel and you had some issues?"

Jim spoke up. "Yeah, Lucky kept looking back. Every time the sled creaked or went through an ice patch, he tucked his tail and didn't like all the noise. He was so busy looking backward that it was hard for him to run forward."

John continued, "You're on Marcus' team, right? Tomorrow he'll switch him back to Team and get a seasoned Wheel dog in. You have to have the right dogs in Wheel. They are close to the sled. It can be noisy and frightening—so they have to have the right temperament. Good ones really help turn the sled and they are the anchor for the team, but they have to be seasoned and understand you're not angry or yelling at them—when you're really just trying to make sure that your Lead dog can hear you way up front.

"Tell me the names of your Lead dogs. Does anybody remember the names of the dogs that ran on your teams?"

We all shouted the names of our Lead dogs with pride, almost as if we were calling out the names of our kids or awards we had won, badges of honor.

"Lead dogs are a lot of fun," John said, followed by a kissing sound and a quick "JAKE!"

He turned and barely had time to set down his drink before Jake came running to him, holding his head up and accepting the affection with almost a gleeful smile.

"They love to pull and can't wait to get out on the trail, where they really shine. They help sniff out the trail. When conditions warrant it, they take direction from the musher, keep the pace in the team and try to keep the gang line tight at all times." John spoke with affection about Jake. "There's been more than one time that Jake has helped me out of a situation.

"Mushers become very attached to their Lead dogs, and because of their role in the team, we keep them close to us. We need to have a relationship where we both know what the other is thinking and an incredible amount of mutual trust." John stopped for a moment as he made eye contact with Jake and continued to playfully rub his head.

Rob spoke up and asked, "What makes a good Lead dog?"

John looking up from Jake said, "Good Lead dogs are smart, have initiative, have common sense, and possess the ability to perform even in less than ideal conditions."

"How can you tell if a dog will be good in Lead?" Rob followed up.

John explained, "Some will take that initiative pretty early, sometimes it's a gut feeling—and sometimes you're put in a situation of having to use a dog in Lead—and they surprise you.

Every year a musher's Lead dogs have something that happens—they get sick or fight with the dog next to them—or if you don't pay attention to their health, they get a cracked paw

53

and they can't go on. It's in these times that another dog gets a chance to step up and take Lead—some don't cut it—and you try another. Some surprise the heck out of you and run like the wind.

**The very best teams have players
that can operate in other positions.
The Lead can be a burdensome place
that wears, wearies, and stresses.
If the Swing dogs can be rotated
with the Lead dogs—
both sets will remain fresh
and the results will show.**

"It's natural for mushers to have their 'leaders in waiting' to run in the next position—which is Swing. These dogs have to be leaders in their own right, and for many, becoming that Lead dog is a natural step," John went on.

"Swing dogs are directly behind the leader, and they key into the leader's moves and translate that to the rest of the team. They 'swing' the rest of the team behind them in turns or curves on the trail. They protect the Lead dogs from attempting a turn—only to find the rest of the team choosing not to follow! They are crucial to making sure everyone makes the journey and stays in sync. You can imagine that if the Lead dogs try to turn GEE and the rest of the team doesn't, it could create big problems.

"Behind these are the Team dogs. They are between the Swing dogs and the Wheelers and add power to the team. In fact, they are the bulk of the team in terms of numbers and power. Settled in between the others, they don't have to be concerned with the stress of leading and the sled is a comfortable distance behind them.

They are free to simply pull with power and run. Not every dog on your team will be a Lead dog—and if you had a team full of Lead dogs, each would be fighting to lead and it would be chaos.

**Not every dog on your team
will be a Lead dog—
and if you had a team full of Lead dogs,
each would be fighting to lead
and it would be chaos**

"This may be more than some of you care to know about the team, but Chris asked the question and I think it's important to understand."

Jason took the opportunity of the pause and spoke up, "If it's all the same to you guys, I'll just stay in Lead, and you guys can worry about who else is behind me!" With that he raised his beer as if to toast the room and took a drink.

The room broke the silence with laughter and a number of us seasoned leaders looked at him with that "yeah, you'll grow up and learn" look.

Nils had been in the room for some time now—just listening and watching. As John turned it over to him, he seemed to cut it short and wrapped up by saying, "And Wheel dogs we mentioned at the start of this conversation, they're the ones that help turn the sled, and they're the ones closest to the sled."

The focus moved to Nils as he talked about tomorrow. "We are going to stick with the pairings as they are—we seemed to get it right for the most part on pairing the mentors with you guys— so in the morning, look for your mentor and get going.

"The plan for tomorrow is to leave here in increments. A different team will leave every 5 to 7 minutes, and we'll time you for fun.

"We have a campsite set up about halfway between here and White Mountain. You'll run your teams to there, and we'll break for lunch. When all teams get in, we'll compare times again—just for fun—and let you know where you stand. We'll take the long way home through a trail we've created for you.

"Tomorrow will serve as a true training run for Thursday. On Thursday we start the three-day run. It's important for you to get some things down tomorrow, so pay attention to your mentor and take in all they have to say. Trust me, you'll need it. Get with them now before you head back to your bunk. They will know when you leave, and they have their plan for you in the morning." With that, a few questions came up. Nils answered a couple of them and then said, "Get with your guide, he'll answer the rest."

I spent some time with Joe, going over the details—when we were going to meet and our strategy. We would be second out. We were going to be first—but with Jason opening his mouth about being Lead dog—they decided to let him go first tomorrow instead.

Joe with his customary sly half smile said, "We'll have fresh powder coming in tonight, and what he doesn't know is that he will be breaking the trail for the rest of us. It will run him a little harder, but we couldn't help ourselves—after that toast."

With that, the meeting broke, and we stood around for a little bit swapping stories and learning more about each other. The fireside room was the perfect place for these nightly debriefs with the atmosphere and warmth of the fire surrounded by the rustic combination of stone and timber. It was a place that calmed you from the day and set the tone for connecting with others.

I stayed for a little while but had so much burning in my heart and running through my head about the dog positions that I wanted to get back and journal before lights out. Tomorrow would be an incredible day—but I didn't want to lose the power of the moment and the dog positions that were an avalanche of illustration.

Unpacking More on
Lead, Swing, Team, and Wheel

Lead Dogs—make sure they are a fit on your team, let them get to know your heart, and keep them close. Learn to develop a mutual intuition and give them access where the rest of the team might not have. Watch for their health, so you don't have to replace them. Make sure their paws are in good shape—in other words, make sure they are free to run without anything hindering their running with all of their potential.

Swing Dogs are like informal leaders in our companies—they are like "Bob." You know, Bob, is the guy that we know has informal power in the group, and we don't want to take our new initiative to Bob, because if Bob doesn't like it, he will start tanking it from the beginning, and we will have no ability to launch effectively. So we take our initiative to every other dog on our team, hoping that the power of the masses—the power of the Team dogs—will overpower Bob's ability to swing the team. Much to our disappointment everyone on the team runs to Bob to ask his opinion anyway.

How can we leverage Bob's popular power? How can we go to our Lead dogs first and then to Bob? Let Bob in on the ground floor, take some of his input into consideration, and let him have a hand in the initiative with myself and the Lead dogs mentoring him. Once this Influencer is on board, Bob will sell the initiative to everyone else. They're going to him anyway, instead of fighting the Swing dog, leverage his capability to swing the rest of the team.

Team Dogs—the bulk of the team just wants to run—they just want to make widgets. They don't want to burn the midnight oil or come in at the crack of dawn. They will never be Lead, and they are fine with that. But you know what? If I didn't have them, we couldn't do what we do. They are vital to every business. We should accept that the office is not their life—that their life is their life—and let them run from 8 to 5 as hard as they can and then clock out and leave it all.

Wheel Dogs—What people are close to me that I allow close to the sled of business? The sled of business is not always pretty. There are things in your business that not every dog needs to see and some dogs will be scared off by. They don't need to handle it. Not everyone needs to know everything—things like cash flow and layoffs and contingency planning. The Team dogs need to run unhindered from the burdens of the sled. Even Wheel dogs that are closest to the sled are still not the sled, and although these Wheel dogs are seasoned confidantes or people you count on to help you turn the business, they're not meant to be pack mules to carry your emotional burdens.

Now I more clearly understand what happened with Carlos several years earlier. I thought Carlos was the equivalent of a Wheel dog—mature and a confidante that I could off-load some of the emotional weight and give him insight into the business. When he breached my confidence and went squealing to the other team members and leaders, revealing my thoughts and feelings regarding the merger, I had no idea at the time I had just mistaken a Team dog for a Wheel dog.

If I'm completely honest, I really tried to make him more like my emotional pack mule.

The emotional baggage on the sled needs to stay on the sled. If I need to talk, I need to find another musher!

Checkpoints

Leaders are normally drawn toward and have a greater connection with the Lead dogs or peak performers.

Not every dog on your team will be a Lead dog—and if you had a team full of Lead dogs, each would be fighting to lead and it would be chaos.

The very best teams have players that can operate in other positions. The Lead can be a burdensome place that wears, wearies, and stresses. If the Swing dogs can be rotated with the Lead dogs, both sets will remain fresh and the results will show.

Planning and preparing for Leader Succession is crucial. Knowing potential leaders is critical to overall mission success on the trail.

Knowing the positions my people naturally play and allowing them to run in that position increases their satisfaction and can lead to better team performance.

Having the right expectations about the team and their respective roles can reduce stress on relational friction.

All positions are important and critical to race success.

Pairing the right learner to the right mentor is an important step to successful growth and mentor satisfaction.

Reflections

On my team, who consistently runs Lead? Swing? Team? Wheel?

Who are my Lead dogs in waiting? How can I start to develop my bench strength for my Lead dogs—in case one goes down?

Do I tend to overuse my Lead dogs or high performers? How can I spread projects out to give others more opportunity and my Lead dogs a breather?

How can I strategically leverage the Swing dogs in my organization?

How can I leverage this Swing dog concept to reach potential clients as well as existing customers?

Do I accept my Team dogs and appreciate their contribution?

Am I abusing a Team dog by bringing them too close to the sled of my business?

5

Building and Running the Team

*When leading a new team, take time to
get to know each of the players personally,
preferably before everyone starts running.*

J oe was right. As I looked outside I could see that when the
front blew through last night, it dumped another foot of fresh
powder on the ground. I could hear the wind most of the night,
and I wondered how much colder today would be than yesterday
and what effects the wind and snow would have on the sled.

Walking into the mess hall, Joe already had his coffee and
breakfast, and I noticed two other mushers with their mentors
making plans—everyone seemingly staking their ground in sepa-
rate corners of the room. I grabbed some food from the line and,
knowing I'd be burning a lot of carbs today, I dished myself a
large bowl of oatmeal, grabbed a couple of bananas (one for my
jacket for later) and I couldn't pass up the smell of the bacon. For
the carnivorous, it was a wall of invitation that instantly made the
mouth water. I found the biggest cup for coffee I could and took
a seat next to Joe.

After a few moments of casual conversation about life and our respective families, Joe said, "I've been thinking about our run today. It's important to consider the run you're going to make before you build your team. This run is going to only be about 30 miles each way. Because we're not going to need a lot of endurance, I think we should add some dogs who are better sprinters to the team."

It's important to consider the run you're going to make before you build your team

---

I thought it sounded logical and asked about the effects of the storm on the conditions and the trail.

"Good thought. That is precisely the reason I lobbied to get the second position today. The first musher out is going to have some tough sledding. That's why I pressed for Jason to go first. Sometimes the young need wisdom added to their zeal." The smirk on Joe's face was priceless.

"When you're running first, in deep snow, you're basically breaking the trail for the rest of the group. If you've ever skied in deep powder, you know what I'm talking about. Once he's packed the trail a little bit, our experience will be much different than his, and we'll be able to have faster times. If we were breaking the trail, I would choose different dogs for the team—dogs that are used to running in deeper snow whose legs were built for endurance."

"That makes sense," I surmised. "I really connected with Oreo and Blue. Is there any way to keep them on the team?" Joe nodded, "Yeah, no problem. We'll add Dizzy and Shadow. I want to add Dale as a Team dog and put her next to Bruce. Dale's only 17 months old, and since this is a training run, I want to see what she can do. We need to add a seventh dog to get you ready for ramping up to eight dogs for the three-day. We'll throw Robbie in for our lone Wheeler."

"Now, it's going to be cold. You need to make sure you have enough layers to run today, still be functional and be fairly comfortable. Get dressed. I'll meet you in the kennel in 10." At that, Joe headed out, I wrapped up breakfast and was off to the mudroom. I had anticipated the cold, so I was already wearing a couple of extra layers.

I met Nils in the coatroom, and he offered his fur-skin hat, the ears wrapped down and tied under the chin. He said, "Out here we go for function over fashion. It may look a little silly, but it will be the warmest thing you can wear on a day like today by far." Not being one to offend the host, I put on the hat and thanked him for the offer. Nils, being ever watchful said, "No exposed skin today. The wind and the cold will cause frostbite very quickly."

Joe was in the tack room grabbing the harnesses and gang line. We went to the sled and quickly went to work without saying much. His team was already set up and on the snow hook. It was time to get mine set and get on the trail. I went first to my Lead dogs, spent a few seconds with each, talking to them and petting them before leading them to the gang line. I introduced myself to the rest of the new team in the same manner. Initially, Blue had an issue with Dizzy being on the team and snapped at her pretty good. After correcting her and telling her to line out, she glanced back at Dizzy but then stayed focused forward, next to the more stoic Oreo.

The morning *was* cold, and today Joe had brought me goggles with the right lenses. I wrapped a wool scarf around my face, double-checking for any exposed areas and could still feel the -30 to -40 degree wind chill cutting through the layers. Risking arrest from the fashion police, I put on the hat from Nils and could not have imagined the difference in warmth.

My adrenaline pulsing, the team was in place, and we were ready to run. Jodie was ready with the countdown to record our starting time that she would then relay to the checkpoint.

What I later learned from Joe was that the countdown was the same as it was for the real Iditarod. It's simply a 5-4-3-2-1 mush. Not a lot of fanfare—and we're off!

Joe took off, and I followed, a little unstable at first but after hitting the trail, everything leveled out. I could definitely see what Joe was talking about after running for just a bit and seeing where Jason had broken the trail. I chuckled to myself and realized that, yes, his day would be more difficult than mine.

My first real scare occurred as we crossed a small hill and were headed down across a ford where the river had iced over. I felt a degree of panic and bewilderment as I looked ahead. Coming out of the powder, you could see cracks in the ice, and I wondered how stable that ice was. As Joe crossed it, I could see the runners of his sled bring water to the surface. As scared as I was to follow into the unknown, he didn't fall through, and I hoped neither would I. As I crossed through I felt as if I had crossed a large sponge. The area sort of gave a little under the sled and then hardened on the return to solid ground. I was thankful to be running second instead of running later in the pack.

**Watch for patches of thin ice—
If possible, watch leaders who
have traveled that path before**

For a while, we just ran. Listening to the sound of nothing was incredible. I purposefully called my dogs by name as we were running, making sure they made a connection to me. I found myself being overly protective of them and watching their rope lines and looking for any signs of vulnerability in the team that was entrusted to me.

The run was great. I could see what Joe was talking about with the sprinters. This was a team that loved to run and loved every second of trying to catch Joe and his team. Getting lost in the enjoyment of watching the dogs run, I was surprised as we approached the checkpoint. Had it been four hours?

As we passed the checkpoint timekeeper, I couldn't help but wonder where our run time would rank in the overall. Joe and I parked the dogs behind the building and were a little surprised to find that Jason and his team had only arrived a minute earlier. We gave the dogs some snacks and threw down a little bit of hay before making our way inside to thaw and get a bite to eat.

Over the next 45 minutes, the remaining teams arrived, some energized and some looking like they were almost ready to quit. Ill-prepared, the weather and the challenges on the trail had almost broken them already, and we were only halfway through our first training run.

Nils tapped his knife against his cup to quiet the room and announced, "At the end of the day, we will announce the winner for the full run, but the front runner at the halfway mark is Chris with a time of 3 hours, 56 minutes, 14 seconds. The rest of the times will be posted on the back door of the mud room. Congratulations, Chris. What was the secret of your run so far?"

Feeling like the credit was due more to Joe than myself, I said, "Building the team seemed crucial, and it was Joe's wisdom to trade out the long-distance runners for sprinters for this run. That proved to be key, and I just want to say thanks to Jason for breaking the trail for me and leaving me clean, packed lines to run in."

It was hard to tell if Jason's face was red from blushing or just red from the cold.

Rob chimed in, "Go get 'em, Lead dog!"

"Mark, you were dead last. What happened?" Nils inquired.

Mark, in his frustrated voice, said, "Man, I just had a couple of dogs on the team that spent more time fighting each other than pulling the sled. It seemed like a great couple of dogs, and for a little bit it was. But the more time they spent next to each other, the more irritated they got at each other. And before long, we weren't making much forward progress. They were in the Team position, and they were pretty much just dead weight that the Lead and Swing were trying to pull. My Leads kept looking back to see what was going on, and my Wheel kept running into the back of the two that were fighting."

When teaming your dogs together— or your people—considering personality and temperament are key

"Sounds like my St. Petersburg office," Gary blurted. Everybody chuckled, and Nils said, "Gary, we need to hear this one. Go on."

Gary seemed surprised that he had said it out loud but went on. "I had great guys that were great team players in other offices, so we put them together to run St. Petersburg. They seemed like a dream team. But they spent more time fighting each other than fighting for business. Turned out Steve, who we brought in from Philly, was more of an analytic, and Don was more of an expressive type, and when you get those two together, sales and engineering don't talk very well.

"The entire office was so caught up in choosing sides or trying to be peacemakers that everything came to a grinding halt. The staff that had once been effective prior to these two being matched up no longer functioned as a team at all. Until this moment, I blamed them for their inability to make it work, when in reality, maybe it's on me for not considering the personalities of the people on the team and how they would interact.

"I've now got a Lead dog who is being pulled down by these two—well, I guess they're more like Swing dogs than Team dogs. It is something that I need to deal with when I get back."

I pulled out the mini-journal from my pocket and made a note to think about this later tonight.

With that, Nils said, "All right guys, let's wrap up. Let's make the trip back home. You'll leave out in the order of your time ranking. Mark, although you left 5th, you came in last, so that changes how you leave out. So you don't have the same problem on the way back, Judy runs better with Fatty, so let me swap dogs with you so you'll have a better run on the way home. Remember what Joe said, 'They can feel your energy.' Try being more confident and assertive."

Everybody packed up and headed out, with me leading the pack.

I was expecting the difficulty of the long way back, and it almost seemed fair that I would now be breaking trail for everybody else when Nils approached Joe and said, "Let's take the same route home instead of the longer route we had planned. The weather coming in is going to turn for the worse, and I'll feel better getting these guys back quicker." Joe nodded in agreement, and just before the timekeeper counted us down again, Joe turned to me and said, "You're leading the way back home. I'll follow you this time." Being apprehensive, I pushed back and said, "No way." Joe said, "You're ready. The trail is marked out. It's the same way back home and I'll be behind you." With my heart pumping loudly, the 3-2-1 countdown almost seemed surreal, and I barely remember pulling the hook, but it seemed like the dogs took off like a shot.

I'm getting the hang of this. It is starting to feel more natural. It seems like on the way back though there are a lot more uphills than I remember. I'm finding myself having to run next to the sled at times or help push the sled with one leg—a tricky move considering, in order to push, both legs have to be on one runner, and balance is essential.

By midafternoon, my legs were really burning, and I was wondering how the real Iditarod mushers do it for hours and hours on end over several weeks. Just as I was lost in that thought, I felt the presence of another team behind me. Not wanting to be passed, I called Blue and Oreo's names, gave them the kissing sound and yelled, "Hike!" The entire team picked up the pace, and it was exhilarating. As I navigated the landscape, it was tricky to try to catch a glimpse of who the rider was that was approaching. Around a turn, I was able to get enough of a view to determine it was Joe, wanting to push me and see how I responded under pressure.

I can say that, to date, there have been very few times that I've felt the level of personal satisfaction and accomplishment as when I pulled into the kennel that night. Being cold, feeling like I was half frozen, dealing with sub-zero temperatures never experienced in Texas, legs burning from strain, face burning from the effects of the wind, and yet a deep sense of achievement. Yes, this was a near perfect day.

After going through the routine with the dogs, showering and changing clothes, we all congregated for dinner and then back to the fireside. The physical exertion, the hot shower, eating a great meal and taking in the atmosphere around the fireside all combined to make for an incredibly relaxed group. You could tell by looking around the room there wouldn't be any late-nighters pulled tonight.

As Nils announced the winners, he began with news that Mark had dropped out and would be heading home. We all liked Mark, but it just seemed like the infighting of his team, the weather conditions, and his own apprehension proved to be too much.

We then learned that Gary had posted the best time for the second run at 4 hours 6 minutes and 2 seconds, seemingly reenergized by his revelations about his St. Petersburg team. My time was second best at 4 hours 9 minutes and 37 seconds. My combined times, however, held up for first, but only 70 seconds separated us from second.

Joe leaned over to me and whispered, "You know if I wouldn't have pushed you, you'd be sitting in second right now." I nodded approval with a smile.

Mentors stretch their protégés— taking them out of their comfort zone when they believe they're ready

---

"Congratulations to all of you who completed the training run. You ran today in less than ideal conditions. Training runs are essential to winning races. Today, we ran the dogs four hours, stopped for lunch, and ran them another four. Iditarod mushers may run their teams twice that in a day, and the key is running longer training runs. If you run your dogs for 10 to 12 hours in a training run, it will seem normal to run that in the race.

"We need to cut tonight short. We've got a very long three days ahead of us, and you guys need to pack for the journey. You all have a list, pack your gear, and we'll see you in the morning in the tack room at 7 sharp."

I sat in the great room for a few moments after most of the group left. Propping my feet up on the brick ledge built up around the base of the firepit, I soaked in the moment, losing myself in the flicker of the fire. I replayed the day's events.

Inspired by the day and the rugged ambiance of the room, I pulled the little booklet and a pen from my pants pocket to capture the life experience and record the wisdom gleaned from the day's mushing.

Checkpoints

When leading a new team, take time to get to know each of the players personally, preferably before everyone starts running.

Watch for patches of thin ice. If possible, watch leaders who have traveled that path before.

When teaming your dogs together—or your people—considering personality and temperament are key.

Mentors stretch their protégés—taking them out of their comfort zone when they believe they're ready.

Training runs are essential to winning races.

Reflections

Am I training my team on how they need to perform in "our" race? Am I treating each race as a new race or just like the last one? What do I need to change to have greater success?

You build the team with the project or run in mind, having the right players for the right journey makes all the difference in the world. How good am I in building my best teams? What team players need shifting to be more effective? What team members need to be moved to other teams?

Sometimes starting second just means you get to run on packed snow, and the journey is a little easier. Am I using the experiences of those before me when planning my route? Am I learning from their mistakes and capitalizing on their successes?

When I win, I don't feel the wind burn. When I lose, I feel everything.

6

Strategies and
Checkpoints

*Make sure to put the dogs before the sled,
not the sled before the dogs—
develop a vision,
and break it into simple pieces
before just acting.*

I awoke this morning to the most incredible Alaskan sky. The front had blown through, and the blue skies were just dotted with clouds.

We all ate a hearty breakfast not knowing what our meals would look like for the next three days. It was noisy with all the activity of everyone being there at once. The energy in the room was at an all-time high. You could feel it.

In the middle of the meal, Nils brought the room to attention. "Hey guys, I know you're finishing your meal. It looks like you are having a hearty breakfast. That's a great decision except for the fact there are no restrooms on the trail until you get to the checkpoints.

"Before we head out this morning, we want to talk to you about where we've been the last couple of days and where we're going in the next few. And then, I've got a surprise for you.

"Over the last few days, you've learned to be in the sled, you've been tethered behind the sled, and yesterday, you ran your own teams. Those of you remaining have overcome some obstacles and fought through some cold. Over the next couple of days, you're going to see that multiply. The cold will seem colder when you know it's not a day trip, and the obstacles will seem more ominous. I guarantee you at least once in the next three days, you will want to quit. If you look around the room at the empty spaces, some already have. History tells me we will have a few more before the end.

"You learned about the dogs and their positions, and some of you learned firsthand about how having a dog in the wrong position can disrupt the whole team. And a few of you have even taken some face plants, like Chris on the first day."

Now my face was turning red and everyone was having a laugh at my expense. After being on a high from my first place finish in yesterday's training run, Nils had definitely brought me back to Earth. I guess I deserved it after the tongue in cheek shot at Jason about breaking the trail for all of us.

"You've learned your GEE from your HAW, a gang line from a tug line, and hopefully you know your Lead dog from your Wheel dog. If not, you might want to hang out here at the lodge for the next couple of days," Nils continued.

"Over the next three days, you're going to need perseverance, strategy and a little luck to make it through to the end. We'll have a couple of awards at the finish. Suffice it to say, first one in and last one in are obviously two awards. The other two are subjective, and the mentors will decide those.

"So to get you going, I have an incredible treat for you guys. One of the leaders in our sport that has run the race for years has had many top 10 finishes and runs a successful kennel near Talkeetna, and is here with us today. The way this person runs their races and their business is studied by learners and leaders alike. I know you'll learn a lot from this person, so please welcome Lizzie Hans-Haecker."

There was more than one mouth that dropped as this five-foot-nothing female stepped to the front of the room in a bright pink coat, holding a puppy. I hate to seem judgmental, but I don't know if any of us expected her from his introduction.

"Gentlemen, I can tell by the look on your faces that you're all stunned. I don't think any of you expected a female musher to be brought in to discuss strategy for your three-day adventure," Lizzie said. I think we were all equally shocked that she projected a strong confidence about her and had seemingly no qualms about commanding a roomful of men.

"Let me congratulate you, Chris, for your win yesterday." In a more playful tone, she added, "Female mushers in Alaska have a saying inspired by Susan Butcher and Libby Riddles that goes like this, 'Alaska, where the men are men and women win the Iditarod.' So when you're ready for some real competition, let me know, and I'll race you. I'll even give you a head start."

Ah! When you're out front, you're everybody's target. Once again I'm blushing as laughter breaks out and almost wishing I had come up in second . . . almost.

"But seriously, I want to talk to you now about your strategy and the strategy process we go through as mushers preparing for the Iditarod. Obviously, I'm not going to give away all my trade secrets, but I'll give you enough to keep up with me.

"Our first strategy is to make sure we have a great team. At my kennel, we're constantly raising the next generation of great race dogs." Lizzie raises the puppy that she's holding and says, "Like her. This is Sasha. It's not that I haven't bought any race-ready dogs, but I prefer to raise them from pups so along with *their* DNA, they have *my* DNA." She turns and hands Sasha to a helper, takes off her coat, and hands that to him, as well. She picked back up without missing a beat. "We go through a lot of trouble to make sure we have the right dogs, and we put them in the right spots on the team. I understand you've learned a little bit about that already."

**Our organizations should be
like Lizzie's kennel—
building the next generation of
leaders from the ground up**

"In the planning stages for the Iditarod, you *have to be* a forward-thinker. There are 26 checkpoints and months before the race, you have to plan your food and supply needs and ship them ahead to each checkpoint. Obviously, without the right food and supplies for you and your team, you're not going to get very far. You have to ship enough food and supplies for 16 dogs and yourself, and that doesn't happen without forethought.

"Guys, not to diminish what you did yesterday, but this isn't a day trip. You already know that the Iditarod is a marathon—1100 miles of frozen Alaskan landscape. Double the hours and then multiply what you did yesterday times two weeks. Then you will have a rough idea, and you didn't even do the planning, training or logistics. You just ran.

"To warn you, it is a full-blown addiction. I don't know if they have Iditarod Anonymous yet, but let me be the first member. 'Hi, I'm Lizzie, and I'm addicted to the adrenaline of the Iditarod.'" As that caused a break in her speaking, I looked around the room and was surprised at the level of engagement in this testosterone-filled dining hall.

Lizzie continued, "Let me give you an acronym for race success. The acronym is RACE, and we use RACE to walk through the steps and to teach protégé mushers a process that is proven for race effectiveness.

R.A.C.E. for Success

"The **R in RACE stands for Ready**. Obviously, there is a ton of things that go under Ready—things like What's our vision? How will we run the race? How far will we go before we rest? What does my team look like? What is my team best at? Is my team this year made up of sprinters or long-distance runners? What do I know about my competitors and their teams? What's the weather going to be like? Are there any advances in sled technology that we need to look at? And this just scratches the surface of all that goes into us being RACE Ready.

"The **A stands for Action**. This is the part where we work the plan and we get the team members doing their part. The best race strategy left in the lodge and not implemented is always trumped by a marginal strategy implemented to the fullest. Guys, in my kennel and on my team, I emphasize simplicity and Action. Without Action, we're just thoughts, without simplicity, it will never get out of the kennel. Your dogs need simplicity. And they need a job to do—they are happiest when they have a job to do. It's dogs before sled, not sled before dogs. It's simplicity and Action. I had a mentor a long time ago tell me, 'Lizzie, I'm not judging you on your intentions or your efforts, I'm judging you on your outcome.' I thought it was hard at the time, but it has served me extremely well over the years.

"The **C stands for Checkpoints**. Again, you may or may not know, but there are 26 checkpoints in the Iditarod. All serve a purpose, and there's no way we could in our minds run 1100 miles. So, it helps when we break it up into 20 to 26 training runs, and that's something that our dogs even know is very achievable. For each segment, the terrain is different. That piece of the journey stands on its own. At each Checkpoint, or at the end of each segment, you need to take the time to evaluate your experience over that terrain and record the lessons learned so that you can run the race better next time.

"Finally, the **E stands for Evolve**. If you fail to evolve, if you fail to change, if you fail to adapt, you will die. It happens in creation, it happens in careers, and it happens on the trail. Evolve is where you look at the information you learned at the Checkpoints and your evaluated experiences, and you implement it. You immediately put it to use in your daily running."

My head is spinning. My journal has been out of my pocket for the last few minutes, and I can't write fast enough for the thoughts to come out of my head. How can there be so much business wisdom in her words. She's talking about dogs and mushing and yet carrying more business wisdom than I've heard in $1,000-a-day seminars.

Lizzie's voice brought me back to attention. "Guys, this content is a multi-week mushing course I teach at the kennel, but Nils thought this snapshot would add great value to your experience. I trust you have already spent time with your mentors and discussed your strategy. But I'm here to offer up kibbles of wisdom to any questions you may have. I don't want to hold you guys up because I know you want to get on with your adventure, but I do want to take a few questions before we cut. Who has a question?"

A voice immediately asked, "So who's the fastest musher in the Iditarod today?" Lizzie responds, "You're what, 25?" Jason says, "Twenty-four. What does that have to do with my question?"

"I've got a lot of young mushers that come into my kennel and ask the same question. I can give you the answer to 'who's the fastest' and the technology that's making them run better times, but if I can give you a little counsel, the race doesn't always go to the fastest. It goes to the one who finishes first. The one that endures. In order to be the fastest, you first have to finish. So let me give you some of my keys to finishing: leading your team, managing their energy, deciding when you're going to rest them, and capitalizing on momentum. That's what wins races."

The race doesn't always go to the fastest— It goes to the one who finishes first

Gary, who I've noticed has rejuvenated since we first met, asked, "As a seasoned musher, what are some signs that tell you that you need to deviate from your strategy? I believe you called it 'evolve.'"

"Great question," Lizzie said. "If I could be a little crude, we have a saying on the trail that dead dogs don't mush. If your plan's not working, you have to adjust. You cannot continue to beat a dead horse or, as we call it, run a dead dog. Sometimes I make changes to the team, and sometimes I make changes to me or my plan.

"The condition of the team impacts the strategy. Some dogs might be fighting illness. Do I need to drop them? Are there dogs not pulling their weight or who are causing problems with the other dogs? Last year, Bernie, my Lead dog, just wasn't in the game. She wasn't running. So I pulled her and put her on the sled. At the next stop, I put her back in her position, and she snapped out of it. She knew she didn't want to be back in the sled with the rest of the team recognizing she wasn't running."

Now my interest was piqued and I asked, "So, wait a minute. Is it hard for you to drop a dog?"

Sometimes you have to drop a team member if it's hurting the rest of the team— If you don't, the whole team suffers

Lizzie replied, "Make no mistake about it, I love my dogs, I'm committed to my team. But if a dog is not performing, or it's in their best interest health-wise to drop them, I have to drop them. Regardless of my feelings, I'm not willing to sacrifice the rest of the team, or the race, for one dog. I have to make the hard decisions, and it's just a part of mushing.

"Adjustments with me or my plan are going to relate to conditions on the trail such as bad weather. Is another competitor pushing me? Is the trail icy or snow covered? Or even, is there a lack of snow? In recent years, we've had a lack of snow on some parts of the trail. If you have any of these conditions, and you don't evolve your plan of action, you won't win. Pure and simple. In some cases, you may not even finish the race."

With that, Nils stepped back in. "Lizzie, you're awesome. Let's thank Lizzie for her time and wisdom today." The group applauded as Lizzie waved and exited the mess hall. Nils then gave us a 30 minute warning before take-off by saying, "Get with your mentor to find out the order in which you're leaving. The first musher leaves out in 30 minutes. It looks like it's going to be a great day."

I walked across the room to talk to Joe and found out we had drawn last straw. We wouldn't leave for another hour and five minutes. Still swimming in my own thoughts from Lizzie, I sat back down and took advantage of the time to tie up some notes in my journal and get my head out of business and back into mushing.

Checkpoints

Getting RACE ready:

R — ready
A — action
C — checkpoints
E — evolve

Make sure to put the dogs before the sled, not the sled before the dogs—develop a vision, and break it into simple pieces before just acting.

Our organizations should be like Lizzie's kennel; building the next generation of leaders from the ground up.

Our teams need to be able to run with simplicity.

Sometimes you have to drop a team member if it's hurting the rest of the team. If you don't, the whole team suffers.

Reflections

On large projects, am I breaking it down into smaller pieces? Am I debriefing after each segment and making adjustments as needed before tackling the next piece?

How am I judging my team members?
By their intentions? Or by their results?

7

Challenges, Problems and Solutions

Adversity is life squeezing you like a sponge—
what is in you is bound to come out.

hat a difference a day makes . . .

The exhilarating high of coming in first for the training run was quickly turned to angst.

Before we even got out of the kennel, we found a stanchion on the side of the sled was broken and had to make immediate repairs. After 15 minutes of working on it, Joe asked John if he could get another sled for me to run on. John left out in the direction of the tack room and returned with the sled that Mark had used before dropping out. I wondered if that was a sign or omen of something to come. I'm going to use a sled from a dropout for the next three days and I'm feeling a little superstitious.

Trading out the sled, I couldn't help but wonder what effect this was having on the dogs—to be attached to one sled—only to be trading it out for another. I knew the dogs were anxious to run, and so was I. We were losing precious minutes. To top it off,

Nils was prophetic in his statement at breakfast. I had eaten too much. The energy, stress and breakfast had all come together and I wasn't feeling that well.

Joe must have seen something on my face that clued him in to where I was. He stopped in the middle of our activity of swapping the sleds, made a deliberate point to walk over to me and said, "You're going to have to change your mind-set before we start. Things happen—things will always happen. Go inside, use the restroom, put some cold water on your face and shake it off. We can't have the dogs feeling your downbeat energy—it's not good for the team."

My mind was still racing a thousand miles an hour with all of the issues of the morning. I was allowing my mind to play the negative movie that seems all too familiar. I used the shock of the cold water from the sink to break my thought patterns. By the third or fourth splash, I was purposefully managing my inner self-talk and gaining control of my attitude.

"Everyone faces adversity."
"It's not what happens to me, it's what happens in me."

I came back into the kennel fully reset in my resolve and determined to project a positive attitude. I took time to address each dog on the team, petting their heads, gently patting their sides, calling each by name and encouraging each with a mini pep talk. I don't know if they needed it or not—but I needed to do it.

As the timekeeper counted down to zero, we took off from the kennel. The replacement sled had a different feel, a different weight balance. Having taken on an 8th dog now, I was nervous.

On each sled there are two ways to slow or stop your team— one is the brake (a metal U-shaped bar with a spike on each side that bites into the snow when stepped on), and the other is the drag. I can only equate the drag to a small rubber car mat. It fits between the runners, much like the brake, but it is a much more fluid way to slow the team. Small teeth on the underside of the mat create drag—and the more weight placed on the mat, the more drag created for the team.

I thought that it would be better to start out of the gate slow and that I should control my team with a tight rein (or tight brake) and then let them ease out, much like applying more gas and less clutch. My theory didn't take long to test. As we were leaving the kennel, I was too much on the brake. At the first turn, the dogs went left, my weight shifted right, and my foot on the break caused the right spike to bite hard. In a blink, the sled lurched and flipped, slamming me hard to the ground. My right shoulder landed first and the sled was nearly wrenched from my hands. I'm now frantic, already desperate to regain the time that we had just lost, and now holding on with a team that's ready to pull with all they have.

Thankfully, Joe looked back, stopped his team, and caught Blue and Oreo as the team pulled up next to him. I quickly righted the sled and pushed to take off, trying desperately to project a calm exterior for the team and my mentor. Internally, my mind was a blur. I'm disheveled, cold, embarrassed, and furious at myself.

It took several miles of self-talk to drop the fixation on failure and flipping the sled. I continuously fought each thought of failure with something I had learned from one of my business mentors, John Maxwell. "Forget the failure, learn the lesson." It felt as if I repeated this a thousand times before moving on.

Forget the failure, learn the lesson!

The rest of the morning run was an improvement from the start, but starting last is always tough sledding. I was still learning the new sled and the dogs on the team, watching their dynamics and wondering if I had worn them out from my missteps at the start.

Nursing the sore shoulder, I leaned on my guide and mentor a lot that first day. Joe had helped me through that rough start, and I was glad to have his coaching on the strategy that we were going to run with. We made it through the 3 checkpoints of the day and were able to shave a little time off, although we had a tremendous gap to try and close.

That night at the first overnight campsite I learned that others had not been without their issues either—there were stories of sickness in dogs and mushers, equipment issues and wrong turns.

The second day proved to be one of the most challenging of my life. Problems and personal adversity seemed to be lurking around every corner. I have felt that it is trite to use the phrase, "What doesn't kill you only makes you stronger," and yet I found myself using that to keep me moving forward.

The toughest part of the journey was going over Gus Pass and down through Rondy Falls. The winds over the pass are horrific, blowing snow, creating difficult visibility and the temperature is easily 25 degrees colder as a result of the wind chill. The conditions showed us no favoritism as the sun and the blowing snow combined for brutal visibility, leaving me no choice but to rely on my team and trust that they knew the trail and could sense the right direction.

Rondy Falls is on the back side of Gus Pass. It is a steep and icy descent that has several drop downs that makes you feel as if you are mushing your team down a flight of stairs. Each step landing the sled with a thud, shaking everything, jarring everything and reverberating stress on the kidneys and, in my case, my shoulder. There could not have been a worse position to be running than last going through Rondy Falls. The setting sun cast large shadows across the icy path, and as the sun fell, so did the temperature. With both dropping fast, coyotes began calling to each other. Our intensity and alertness heightened as the echoing howls moved closer than was comfortable. The other sleds in front of us—all with novice mushers, like myself, had proven to be brutal on the condition of the trail. The steep descent had caused everyone to stand on their brakes hard and had caused ruts in the snow and ice that were 8–10" deep in places. On the last step down, with darkness having closed in around us, a hinge on my brake came loose, throwing my right runner against the wall of the rut. My stomach sank as I heard a crack.

As soon as it was safe, I parked the team to look at the damage. My shoulder throbbing from the pounding and wrangling of the sled for the last two hours, I inspected the sled. My right runner was broken.

Have you ever seen any of the movies where the guy on the sidewalk gets drenched by a car driving through a puddle near him? Imagine how he feels . . . That's how I felt inside when in the middle of assessing the damage on the sled as the weather started to alternate from a thick, wet snow into a miserable freezing rain. Everything was soaked and literally ice cold!

How do they do it? How do they make 1100 miles? I'm struggling after two days—they last 10 days over worse terrain. I grabbed a couple Excedrin and threw them back with a quick gulp of water.

Did I really expect this to be easy and to sail through it without having challenges?

Was I so naïve to think that my early win would exempt me from any of this?

As I was being swallowed in self-doubt and pity, teetering on the edge of throwing in the towel, Joe stepped in.

"So what?"

"What do you mean 'So what?'" I shot back.

"So what? It's cold. It's hard. Your shoulder hurts. You broke a runner. SO WHAT?" Joe said as if it was all insignificant.

"You teach people about business, right? Aren't there problems in business?

"We have a saying out here that frustration comes from your expectations. If you expected to run a race and be problem free—you're going to be frustrated. This is how racing is—this is how life is—you face problems.

Frustration comes from unrealistic expectations

"One year on the trail, we had a blizzard come in. I couldn't even see to the front of my Team dogs. I stopped them and created places where they could at least have some break from the blowing snow, and then I did what my father had taught me. I knelt down in the snow and I faced the storm."

"You didn't turn your back to the storm?" I inquired.

"No! You must turn your face to the storm. In this position, it causes the snow to blow around you and pile up behind you. It forms a mound that you can then dig into and create a shelter. You can hollow it out, like a miniature igloo, and last for a couple of days.

"If you turn your back to the storms, you will be covered and most likely die. But facing the storms creates a place of refuge.

"What do you teach businesspeople? Don't you teach people some of these things?"

My mind immediately went to a large framed picture that I had heard hangs in the boardroom of a Fortune 500 company. The sign reads, "PROBLEMS ARE MONEY. SOLVE THE PROBLEMS, AND YOU GET THE MONEY."

I said, "Yeah, I do. But I'll tell you about that when we break for camp tonight. For now, let's get going. We have a race to finish!"

Joe smiled with satisfaction that he'd gotten through to me, broken my mental spiral, pulled me out of my rut of self-pity and got me pointed back to the trail. I changed out the batteries in my headlamp and, now, everything was a little brighter.

I rode the rest of the night with my weight on the left runner. I was drenched and half frozen but thankful for Joe's support in bolstering the mind-set that I could overcome what seemed to be relentless and overwhelming problems.

I thought often over the next 30 miles about Lance Mackey. He had gone through throat cancer, had a good chunk of his throat cut out, had lost part of his saliva glands and had to carry a water bottle just to keep his throat moist. Only three years later, in the 2007 race, he went 200 miles on a broken runner and WON!

At the campsite that night, I learned that Rob and Mitch had dropped out, and they were taking a helicopter back to the lodge. Mitch just called it quits, and Rob had broken a runner in the same place we had. I thought about how that could easily have been me had I not been willing to stop and refocus.

That night over dinner the three of us that remained and our mentors talked about the issues. Gary and I had a long conversation about belief windows. I shared with him the sunglass principle and how the sunglasses and goggles that Joe had lent me *did* affect how I saw the trail.

Jason, to my surprise, jumped in to talk about how the concept had helped him in sales. That when he saw other sales guys seeing a situation as impossible, he chose that point to decide that it was possible and take advantage of their limiting beliefs.

I'm reminded of how deep it can become embedded in us—and how the concept really is true—that none of us sees reality. We all see our own reality. How true it is what Jim said after the first day, "If you think you can or think you can't, then you're probably right."

Gary had years of experience and wisdom that came out that night, and I was surprised at how much he was willing to share compared to previous nights at the fireside.

I think one of the biggest aha's that I took from Gary that night was when he said, **"Problems are not the problem—the problem is that we can't handle the problem, can't talk about the problem, can't work together to solve the problem—so the problem is not the problem. We're the problem."**

As we were talking, I paused for a minute to ask Nils and Joe if I could bring Blue into the yurt. She was an incredible Lead dog today and with all the challenges had really proven herself. So for the rest of the conversation, Blue was right there with me as we discussed life, adventure, and business. I had only met this dog a couple days earlier, but I was feeling drawn and connected to her.

Worn out from the day, I decided to turn in. I put down a little straw next to my cot for Blue, grabbed my journal and captured some thoughts from the day.

Checkpoints

Adversity is life squeezing you like a sponge—
what is in you is bound to come out.

Frustration comes from unrealistic expectations

Forget the failure, learn the lesson!

If you turn your back to the storms, you will be
covered and most likely die. But facing the storms
creates a place of refuge.

Problems are money. Solve the problems,
and you get the money.

Problems are not the problem—the problem is
that we can't handle the problem, can't talk about
the problem, can't work together to solve the
problem—so the problem is not the problem.
We're the problem.

Overcoming adversity or giving into adversity—both
create momentum.

Reflections

When trouble hits me—What are my beliefs? What is my response?

Do I play the movie in my head that connects the present situation to everything that's ever gone wrong? Do I connect unrelated dots to form a picture of the worst case scenario instead of the possibilities?

What storms do I need to turn my face to, back home?

As a leader, I don't have the luxury of wallowing in self-pity or being frustrated. It will transfer to the team and crush the will to go forward.

8

Performance and a Little Trick-Foolery

Like most things in life,
"You snooze, you lose!"

I was awake early and looked around the room. In the dim light, I could make out that it looked like everyone except John was still in their cots. As John was Gary's mentor, I just assumed that he was out tending to the dogs or checking on an animal sound. Gary's food cooler was still in front of his cot, and I turned over to catch another 10 minutes or so.

My eyes opened again as I was startled awake by the commotion of the teams and everyone throwing their gear together. I asked Joe what was going on, and he said that John and Gary had pulled a "Rick Mackey."

"A what?" I asked confused, still wiping the sleep from my eyes.

"A Rick Mackey. Back in the day, Rick would take two coolers with him. At some point in one of the races, he snuck out early and left a cooler behind. So that no one would suspect he was gone, he put pillows under the covers and left one of his coolers to make it look like he was still sleeping.

"John and Gary have a 40-minute head start."

Hastily, we packed our sleds, snacked the dogs and headed out. Jason and Hugh, his mentor, were right behind us having fallen victim as well.

The storm from yesterday was still lingering this morning, but you could tell it would be burning off soon and it would be a great day to run.

The first day Joe had asked that I follow his lead and yesterday we took turns leading. As we started this morning, Joe let me know that I would be leading the entire way back. I shook my head and smiled. Joe was using my own training concept on me! I had mentioned it to him as we were discussing training runs earlier in the week. It is based on the "I do, we do, you do" model. We use it with intensity in training future leaders and even call it "the 90-Day Burn."

There is a lesson that I had learned while being here, and that is the diligence in checking on performance progress. We had a plan that we would average nine miles an hour for the trip back. We thought, before Gary's trickery, that it would give us a chance at coming in first. In order to hold ourselves accountable for reaching this goal, we now agreed to check this every hour on the hour. As we monitored our progress we would know how we needed to make adjustments and would have the information in time to *Evolve* and improve our performance.

Diligence to progress checks allows you to respond and *Evolve* in enough time to better your performance outcome

Jeff and Hugh were still loading their sleds when we left the checkpoint.

During the first leg of the day, I noticed a change in Shadow.

While pulling the sled, the dogs wear booties on their feet, a body harness for the ropes, and coats when they need it for warmth. The booties help keep their paws from cracking and provide a degree of protection. The body harness has two places to connect the neck and tug lines, and it helps even the distribution of pull over more of the dog's body. As the dogs run, the neck line is generally loose and the tug line is tight showing that the dog is pulling the sled.

On Shadow, I began to notice that his neck line was tight and his tug line was loose. I watched this curiously at first, and the more I watched the more it became obvious that Shadow just wasn't in the mood to run well this morning.

I radioed back to Joe and told him what was going on. We went back and forth over the next hour about the situation, and I must have frustrated Joe. He had already given me the solution about a half an hour earlier and I had not yet taken action.

He finally radioed and said, "Chris, when it comes to your team—it's your team. You cannot complain about what you continue to permit."

Boy, that stung.

You cannot complain about what you continue to permit

I pulled the team over and unhooked Shadow. Walking him back to the sled, I made him get in.

To add insult to injury, as we were pulled over to deal with Shadow, Jason and Hugh flew right past us. I couldn't help wonder what would have happened had I just dealt with the problem sooner. Would they have passed us?

It's hard to imagine a dog getting embarrassed, but that seems to be what happened. Shadow was squirming and whimpering and holding his head down. Occasionally, the other dogs would look back as if to say, "What's up with you?" "Don't you know you're supposed to be down here with the team, helping us pull the load and win?"

Teammates have a way of letting other teammates know when they're not pulling their weight

Joe had said that would happen and mentioned that we wouldn't do it for long. Like Lizzie's story, just long enough to let him know he needs to improve, but not too long as to break his spirit. He told a story about Dragon, a Lead dog that was probably too young for the emotional weight of the position and the pressure of the Iditarod, that he thought would make it. He didn't—and to my surprise, Joe said after running a day or two like that, he shipped the dog home. The worst part, he said was that Dragon was never the same.

It reminded me of a quote I heard a month earlier while watching a football game. One of the TV announcers had made a comment that "the NFL breaks more quarterbacks than it makes."

Leaving Shadow in the sled the right amount of time was good for him and the team. I made a mental note to not put potential leaders in places or situations that are too big for them to handle and to look for ways with less risk to grow their potential.

At the next checkpoint, I grabbed extra supplies as Joe and I talked about making a run for it and not stopping until we reached the Lodge.

Joe said, "We will give it our best shot, but watch the dogs. Reading their body language will tell you if they can go all the way. I've trained this team for runs like this, so it should come natural to them. Remember what we said earlier, 'your dogs will race like you've trained them.'"

By this time I had learned my team, I knew each dog fairly well. I knew their strengths and how each was in the positions. I moved Oreo back up to Lead with Blue, put Dizzy and Bruce in Swing, and reconnected Shadow in Team, next to Dale (a young 17-month-old female). In Wheel, I had two faithfuls of the adventure—Fatty and Robbie.

I had learned that Blue and Oreo really responded well to my voice and to verbal encouragement. Dizzy and Bruce had similar personalities, and they ran better when teamed next to each other. I wasn't sure what the extra synergy was about, but I knew enough to know they were better when teamed together.

I was counting on Dale's youthful vigor to add any additional fire needed if Shadow was still a little lagging, and as for the two Wheelers—well, I learned that they love sardines at snack time. Although I didn't care for the smell, I decided the extra effort I got from them was worth the stench.

I was now at ease with the new sled and confident in my mushing. We shot out of the checkpoint with purpose. If I'm honest about my mind-set, I was still working to overcome my belief that a new problem might take us down at any minute.

As we crossed into an open, snow-covered meadow, the team kicked it into high gear and really surged. It was exhilarating, and I had a newfound optimism.

At the last checkpoint, we acknowledged the helper and discovered that Jason and Hugh were parked and that one of Jason's Lead dogs was being examined by the veterinarian. We had no idea what had happened but trusted they were in good care and wanted desperately to catch Gary.

We tossed a couple of snacks to the team, some sardines to the Wheelers and, capitalizing on the momentum, took off again.

To my amazement, Dale (the 17-month-old female running in Team with Shadow) ran the rest of the way to the lodge as far out to the left as she could go. I couldn't help but remember what John had said about sometimes leaders revealing themselves. She wasn't having any part of running behind Dizzy. Even though she wasn't running lead that day, you couldn't have told her that!

Sometimes young leaders reveal themselves if you pay attention

As the day wore on, I made the extra effort to maintain my consistency of verbal affirmations and an appropriate amount of snack rewards—to keep them going at peak—without spoiling them with gluttony!

About 20 miles out, I radioed to Joe, "What do you think about running ahead of me?"

"Why?" Joe replied. "You're doing fine."

I said, "Your 16 dogs are still stronger and there's more in their gas tank than my 8. I was thinking I might get more out of my team if they were chasing your team."

I didn't immediately hear back from Joe and was wondering about his response when I heard them on my heels.

Joe was calling to his team, yelling, "On by!" The power and speed of the 16 was no match for my 8, and they passed us quickly.

Dale and Blue, not liking any part of being passed, barked and pulled harder, picking up the pace of the entire team.

The closer we came to the lodge, the more familiar the dogs were with the trail, and they knew that the finish was not far off.

On the last uphill climb of the day, I hopped off the sled with lungs and legs burning and ran beside the sled while holding on with my right hand. I had no idea where Gary's time was ending up but suspected that whatever was going on with the vet was wrapped up quickly and that Jason was right on my heels. I didn't want to leave any extra seconds on the trail.

The expansive northern sky filled with blues, and streaks of white thin clouds had muted to a dull gray then faded to black. It was dark now, and we had been chasing the lights of the finish area for the last mile or so. The last stretch of trail dumped us out into the street in front of the lodge. Nils had replicated Front Street in Nome and the race to the Burled Arch from the actual Iditarod race. Joe had radioed me to pass him just before we left the trail so that I could cross the finish ahead of him.

We had another 300 yards to go. I don't know what I expected to feel coming into this point, but I was beginning to feel over-whelmed with emotion. I had done it. I didn't quit. I *could* do it.

I've achieved a lot in my life and my career already, but very little compares to the satisfaction of overcoming the adver-sities of the last week—conquering the adventure and myself along the way.

Oreo and Blue seemed to be strutting at this point, as if they knew there was a finish line. Little Dale was still attempting to run Lead from Team, believing that Nils, the staff, and the other spectators were there cheering just for her. They brought me home. We finished the race.

I had conquered myself, conquered the adventure, and finished the race!

I noticed that in the small crowd were a few familiar faces of the guys who quit the race earlier in the week, and I saw that Gary had already made it in. His team was fed, and his equipment already put away. His trick had done the deal. He even had enough time to change clothes and be back before I crossed the finish line to help me celebrate, and to let me know that the old dog still had a few tricks.

After a brief celebration, we turned the team up the drive and into the kennel. Releasing the dogs from their harnesses and letting them run about for a few minutes before kenneling them, I watched as each one ran and wiggled upside down with their back against the snow. Some ran past other dogs and stopped, as if to say, "Do you want to smell the trail? We ran for 3 days! It was great!"

I was so proud of my team. They had given me all they had, and what we accomplished in three days together was beyond what I would have thought possible.

As I got back to the mess hall, I got word that Jason was on his way but was still another half hour out. I'm torn between grabbing a cup of coffee to warm up or having an ice-cold beer. I decided on coffee and to wait for the crab boil later to have a beer, or two, or three. As I sat down with Joe, I asked if he knew what had happened to Jason's team.

Joe responded with concern, "Jason had noticed that one of his Lead dogs, Seavey, wasn't acting right. He had put Seavey in the sled until he could get to the checkpoint. The vet checked him out and said that he had a heart condition and that if he had continued to run it may have killed him."

When the bell rang, announcing the impending arrival of Jason, we all made a beeline for the Arch. As Jason and his team of now seven approached, we cheered and yelled as if it were any of the recent Iditarod winners, King or Mackey or Buser or Jonrowe.

As Jason and Hugh crossed through the Burled Arch, a staffer brought down the Red Lantern and offered it to Jason. He then blew out the flame, signifying the traditional completion of the race. All mushers were home. One last cheer and we all headed up to the lodge.

Back in the mess hall, Nils and the team had prepared a feast of king crab, potatoes, corn, and all the beer we could drink. As tired as we were, I think about two or three was our limit before heading for our last debrief.

This time the fireside meeting was brief as we could hardly hold our eyes open. Tomorrow, we would get to sleep in and anticipate the banquet celebration at lunchtime. All of the pressure was off.

Our bodies ached, and as the embers died on the fire, Nils welcomed us to an elite club that had finished the adventure.

I was too tired to journal tonight. I decided capturing my thoughts would have to wait for breakfast. I pulled at the tape that held the picture of my family on the wall beside my bed. I missed them and was glad that I would be heading home soon. It seemed as if it had been an eternity from the time I had stepped off the helicopter five days earlier.

For the first time in a week, I awakened after sunrise. I had slept hard. There are certain mornings when I feel my age more than others. As I started to get out of bed, this was definitely one of them. In addition to the shoulder, I was keenly aware of many muscles I had apparently neglected, where they were, and how much they hurt. I wondered about the dogs, my team, and how they were doing this morning. Had they been fed yet? Is that somebody else's job now? I still felt responsible.

I threw on some comfortable clothes and my baseball cap, grabbed my journal, and headed down for breakfast. As I entered the mess hall, I recognized Kyle as one of the kennel hands and asked about my team. He said that they had already been fed and watered, and they were full of energy and doing great. Knowing that my team was taken care of, I headed for the chow line.

After a hefty breakfast and some socializing, I grabbed my coffee and found a corner where I could journal.

Checkpoints

Like most things in life, "You snooze, you lose!"

Teammates have a way of letting other teammates know when they're not pulling their weight.

Sometimes young leaders reveal themselves if you pay attention.

Diligence to progress checks allows you to respond and <u>Evolve</u> in enough time to better your performance outcome.

It's your sled. You cannot complain about what you permit.

Make sure all teammates are pulling forward and not impeding progress. If they are impeding progress, acting sooner on a problem allows for more options and could save race positions.

Problems rarely work themselves out. Strategic placement of team members produces the best results.

Reflections

Am I creating an organization that breaks more leaders than it makes?

When I need a little more pull from my team, try letting them chase a team just a little faster or better than themselves.

There are few significant victories without a great team.

Persevere long enough, press forward to the checkered flag—and I gain admission to an exclusive club for those that finish the race!

9

Awards and Awakenings

Leading a team to victory is often the result
of conquering or leading one's self first.

After breakfast, they kicked us out of the mess hall in preparation for the banquet.

I ran back to the room to put my journal away, then bundled up and made my way down to the kennel to reconnect with the team. They seemed genuinely glad to see me, and I felt the same. Still, I enjoyed just being with the dogs, sharing euphoria over our finish, and I made sure to give each of them some individual attention and praise. I even snuck out a sardine or two from the kitchen for Fatty and Robbie. It seemed like just a few minutes had passed when the bell rang signifying the awards banquet would begin in 15 minutes.

I made my way back up the snowy path to my room, washed and headed to the mess hall.

The staff had really transformed the room. It looked more like a 5-star dining room than the mess hall we had been in all week and yet it still had that great lodge feel, the coziness, the smell of the fire burning, the majesty of the hewn logs and river rocks. The stage and podium were set in front using the fireplace as the backdrop, with the chairs and tables facing so everyone had a clear view of all the activity. The room was filled with staff and the other adventurers.

Nils called everyone to attention, and the room fell quiet. He opened up the celebration by announcing that lunch would be served first followed by the awards. He asked for a volunteer to ask a blessing for the food and give thanks for the safety of us all in our journey this week.

I hardly remember the food because I spent so much time connecting with everybody in the room that had been a part of this incredible week and that I might not ever see again. I sat for a while with Nils and his family and truly thanked him for his hospitality and his vision for creating this adventure. I would never forget him.

At the close of lunch, Nils taped his glass and announced the award ceremony would begin in five minutes.

After the break, Nils stepped to the podium and announced the order of awards would be in reverse, starting with the Red Lantern and moving to first place.

Nils opened up by saying, "This year's Red Lantern award really can't be given out without the other award that's going along with it. As you may or may not be aware, the Red Lantern award is given to the last musher in from the trail. We're not sure Jason would still have received the Red Lantern award had he not had the concern and responsiveness to care more for his Lead dog, Seavey, than his finishing position in this race.

"We are happy to report that Seavey is making a recovery from a serious infection he picked up on the trail, and he will live to race another day because of you, Jason, and the work of our great veterinary staff.

"So, in my mind, Jason, your primary award is the Heart of a Musher award. It goes to the person we believe best represented the embodiment of *servant leadership*, which is the truest model for mushers. Please congratulate Jason." As Nils began to clap, we all followed and celebrated Jason's awards.

Jason stepped up to the podium, still maintaining that same athletic swagger from earlier in the week, still posturing as that Lead dog. He started off with a bit of humor, "I'd like to thank all the little people who helped me along the way to my glorious position of . . . well, last place."

As the group quieted down, he continued and had a seriousness about him. "When I started this week, I thought it was all about me and the glory that I could get. I was Top Dog in my sales team, and I enjoyed the awards and recognition that went along with it. I have to admit I stand before you a week later with a deep concern for the team and a realization that you don't finish the race without a lot of support from fantastic people and great teammates.

"I've learned a LOT from my dogs. I can't say whether I'm going to pursue sales leadership as a career, but if I do, I'll be able to lean on a lot of knowledge from this week. Thank you, Hugh, for your patience in putting up with my overzealousness and thinking I knew more than I really did at times. Your lessons will stick with me, and I promise to not let go of some of your secrets on the condition that you lose the picture of me sitting in the sled on Day 1."

Everyone had a great laugh imagining the picture of the Top Dog being humiliated by sitting in the stroller position of the sled, and Jason sat back down near the front of the room, taking his Red Lantern and Heart of a Musher awards with him.

Nils stepped back up and added, "Jason, I would have never thought at the beginning of this week that you would be the one receiving that award today. Your maturity and self-sacrificing behavior on the trail was outstanding. My hat is off to you.

107

Maturity is a choice, not an age

"Our next award is the Broken Sled award, awarded to the musher who's overcome the most adversity and still finished the race. There are many of you, if not all of you, who know the pain of what can go wrong on the trail. The list of things is just about infinite. I want to turn it over to Joe who will present this award."

With that, Joe took his place at the head of the room and addressed the group. "So let's talk about some of this musher's adversity. He started off on the three-day with a broken sled before even leaving the kennel, having to grab a replacement sled that he was unfamiliar with and flipping that sled within 60 seconds of mushing, injuring a shoulder.

"There were bad conditions on the trail, including a whiteout and some viscous crosswinds. As we all know, pulling last straw means traveling through the ruts of all the other contestants and mentors traveling in front of you. On top of that, the brake broke on Rondy Pass, which caused a broken runner during freezing rain conditions. We had gear freeze up and were soaked to the bone. He ran the last 30 miles or so back to the camp that night standing on the left runner. He wanted to quit on Rondy Pass, but he didn't.

"The next day he fought through issues with Shadow, a Team dog who didn't want to run, and showed strong leadership in putting him in the sled. He persevered and finished strong. Please join me in congratulating Chris."

I stepped up and looked at the Broken Sled award and had to laugh. "This is not the award I wanted to have on my desk back home, but I can't say that I would have learned as much about my team or myself if I had gotten my first wish.

"I had a great team and a great mentor. My team inspired me when I needed it, and my mentor supplied a good swift kick when I needed that to." I turned and smiled at Joe, and he raised his beer bottle in acknowledgment.

"I have to tell you a story about Dale. She's a 17-month-old that we had put as a Team dog. On the last day, she didn't want any part of running Team and swung out to the left as far as she could, stretching out her neck and tug line. She ran almost the entire day acting as if she was running Lead from three rows back. I can't tell you for sure where she'll be in the future, but I can tell you she has the heart of a leader.

"Lastly, I have to give credit to Blue. It's funny that the two outstanding members on my team that I want to recognize are both female. But these ladies have stolen my heart and kicked some tail in the process.

"This week has been a gut check for me and my belief in what's a problem and how much I can overcome. If I can overcome flipping the sled and Rondy Pass, I'm pretty sure I can overcome most things I'm going to face back in my consulting business. And more important, I will have a different attitude and perspective about failure and adversity in the future.

"Guys and gals, thanks for making it a memorable week for me. If you ever get down to Texas, I'll treat you to some great barbecue."

With that, I hoisted my Broken Sled award in the air and made my way back to my seat.

Nils stepped back to the podium, quieted the room, and began, "We've saved the best for last. Every race is not without strategy, and I'm not sure if he got this one from Lizzie or not, but as of Day 2, Gary was running third in time. On the morning of Day 3, he took a page out of Rick Mackey's handbook, and he and John snuck out early, leaving a cot stuffed with pillows and a cooler at the foot of his bed. With everyone believing he was still asleep like the rest of them, he and John snuck off at least 45 minutes ahead of the others. It was a great bit of gamesmanship. Some of the old-timers in the race would be proud."

Nils took a quick sip of water and continued, "I wasn't sure what to think of Gary, showing up in a full-length cashmere coat, looking like he belonged more on the cover of *Fortune* magazine than in a Cabella's catalog. I was even more uncertain as to what would make a guy like him want to come all the way to Alaska for an adventure that seemed on the surface so out of character for him. He's come a long way. I can tell you from my first impression, he looks like a new man. Our first-place finisher and winner of this group's Top Musher award goes to Gary."

Gary made his way to the front as he received a standing ovation. Nils was right, he had changed from that first night in the bunkhouse when we first met. Gary shook hands with Nils, accepted the trophy and placed it on the podium for all to see.

"First of all, I want to thank John for being willing to help this old dog show these young pups some new tricks," he said as he chuckled and the crowd laughed. "I felt a little bit like a teenager again sneaking out of the house on a Saturday night."

I don't know what he had planned for his next sentence, but he never got it out. Suddenly, Gary was overcome with emotion. Over the next few minutes, Gary poured out his heart to a room full of people who were complete strangers a week ago. It was the classic tale of executive burnout, chasing long hours and the next rung on the ladder. He was to the point of breaking before coming up here. His first marriage had failed and his second was in deep weeds. He had been disconnected from his children and had lost all passion for the next business deal that used to keep his adrenaline going. When his wife said she was separating from him and staying with friends, it was just too much.

In fact, his brother who realized more than he did that he was at his breaking point, had booked the trip for him and paid for it himself. Gary continued, "My brother Bill simply said, 'Here is your reservation, and you're doing this. You've lost all sense of yourself and you're about to lose a great wife. You have to find a way back. Maybe the Alaskan air will help you clear your head.'

"So, to answer your questions Nils, no, it wasn't my choice to be here. However, I'm really glad I gave in and got on that plane. I've connected more with the guys in this room in a few short days than I have with people back home over the last 10 years. I have a tremendous amount of acquaintances, but honestly, I'm not close to anyone."

The mood in the room shifted drastically, as we were unsure about how to process the stark reality of Gary's life. Just as I was wondering if this was in fact Gary's breakdown, the tone of his speech shifted upwards.

"This week, I really feel like I have done a lot of soul-searching, and it's helped me to look at where I'm disconnected from me, from my authentic values. It is now clear to me that I've been running a race where the cost is too high and the return too low. And for the last few years, I've just been going through the motions anyway.

"On the trail, I've committed myself to a better life and to contribute to the better life of others around me. I want to be a servant musher, not just in business, but as a father and a husband. Don't get me wrong, I now have an incredible vision for reaching into the lives of the people I've been leading for 25+ years on the business side. Instead of my legacy being about the mark I've left on the company, I want my legacy to be on the individuals whom I lead and hopefully provide an example that will keep their life sled out of the ditch. I plan on modeling this when I get back by taking whatever effort is needed to reconnect with my family first.

"I know you guys didn't come here to hear the ramblings of an old man, but let me leave you with these words. Live your life on purpose. Most people, like myself, live their life and look back on it with regrets. Look at the trail of your life every day, What's the next checkpoint and the next checkpoint and the next checkpoint. Run to those checkpoints with purpose, and you won't have to look back with regrets. Thanks."

Gary received a standing ovation as he left the stage.

Great Leaders are concerned about their positive influence, their Legacy

Nils added these words of wisdom. "Gary, you're right on. Thanks. I'd like to tell you that Gary's experience is unique, but there are so many people who *find themselves* out on the trail while mushing. It's a story that's played over and over again. We think we're running the race for public glory when the real prize is that, at the end of the race, we've found that we have something far more important, and that's victory over self. Gary, we wish you well on your trip back home and reconnecting with your family. If you want to come back up and spend a weekend with your wife, we'll reserve the honeymoon suite for you two."

I realized I was going to miss Nils' wit and wisdom.

"Let me remind you that the Iditarod is a commemoration of a life-saving mission to bring serum to Nome from Anchorage to save the children who were dying from diphtheria. The initial race was never about the musher's glory. The mushers and teams gave it all for a people that could never repay them with glory. Life is lived best when it's lived for others. What will your legacy be? The legacy of the men that teamed together to brave the Alaskan wilderness is personified year after year in the Iditarod. How will the memory of you be honored at the end of your race?"

Nils finished by pausing for a moment to allow the effect of that last sentence to sink in. He then made a few closing announcements about how the rest of the day would wrap up,

112

transportation logistics back to the airport in Nome and ended, simply, with, "Be safe going home!"

Very few people left the room quickly. We milled about for an hour or so, not wanting to let go of the moment. I finished packing and brought my gear to the transport van. The driver said it would be another 30 to 45 minutes before he was ready to go.

I used the balance of the time with my team. It was hard to believe what a connection I had formed with the dogs. It wasn't easy to leave them, but I was grateful for what each of them had taught me.

On the way out, I asked the helicopter pilot to circle back for one last look over Nils and the Adventure Lodge. The houses in the kennel gave symmetry to the area, and I turned back for one last glimpse across the Alaskan wilderness that had been my adventure.

Checkpoints

Leading a team to victory is often the result of conquering or leading one's self first.

Winning helps bond the team.

Maturity is a choice, not an age.

Great Leaders are concerned about their positive influence, their Legacy.

Reflections

The best mushers are concerned with the health of individuals on the team. Am I looking for subtle and not-so-subtle signs to make sure no one dies or burns out on the trail? Does it show that I care deeply for my team?

The race of life and connecting authentically to self and our values is the higher race. In fact, failing at that race can knock me out of contention, or at least set you back.

The Ultimate race is not about me, not about my glory. The Ultimate Race is living for and giving to others.

10

Living Your Adventure
(Bloggings and Inspirations)

Adventure is not outside man; it is within.

On the flight home, I looked over my journal and the notes that I had taken during the week. This had definitely been a powerful week. I felt rejuvenated with a new sense of purpose for what I do. My thoughts returned to Gary's breaking down and commitment to reconnecting with his own authentic self. His purposing to give great effort to reconnecting with his wife and children led me to think about my own family and the fact that I have a beautiful wife, amazing children, and about many of my clients and friends that I have connected to deeply. I purposed to make sure that I maintained and deepened my connection to my authentic values and the people that mean the most in my life.

Purpose and destiny are things I don't take lightly. I believe in the spirit in people and that when we decide in our hearts— truly decide—to change our lives or our circumstances, nothing but ourselves can get in the way. I renewed my optimism and committed to owning the mind-set that "problems are not problems, but momentary obstacles that will be a part of our victory speech at the end." Many people want to have great victories in their lives, but they forget that there are no great victories without great battles. People want for others to ask about their great testimonial, but they forget that great testimonials don't come without great tests.

Feeling inspired and wanting to transfer this empowered mind-set to my team and our clients, I opened my laptop and began writing a blog to live by for the rest of the year and for the years ahead. I hope it will be as meaningful to you as it is to me.

BLOG

How adventurous is your life right now? Does your life contain destiny and purpose at this moment?

Over the last week I have gained a fresh perspective on "running" my life race on purpose. I spent the week learning to mush a team of Alaskan huskies. I learned that, although the Lead dog is in front of the team, the true leadership position belongs to the musher. He or she is responsible for the plan, the care of those running the journey with them, and the determination to see it through.

I need to map out or chart my course and then run that course, on purpose. If I am going to experience the success and the life that I want, then I will need to design or create the vision for each of those areas. This means I need to define success—I need to have a mental picture of what I want to see come to pass in both my personal and professional life. Having done that, I need to learn and leverage the power of the people on my team. Let's start with me first. I am the one in control of my sled.

Most of us (myself included) have a tendency to accept what life deals us, rather than to pursue our created destiny.

The word *destiny*, literally means to decide beforehand. This week I had decided beforehand to finish this wilderness adventure. I almost turned my destiny over to the hands of fate.

You see, many people confuse destiny with fate. They believe that "whatever comes my way, that is my destiny."

Can I tell you? That is not destiny—that is default.

That is fatalistically accepting a default value—the fate that comes your way.

The fate on the trail are the problems, breakdowns, and dropouts. Even as I think about my yard back home, the default value on my yard is not lush green grass with incredible flowers and meticulous landscaping. The default value of my yard is weeds! Bland, overgrown, unkempt WEEDS!

It is amazing that we will understand this concept when it comes to some things and yet, somehow, we neglect this concept when it comes to ourselves.

Can I just take a moment to tell you that you and I are worth far more than a meticulously landscaped yard? We have exceeding value FAR beyond that of dirt, grass, mulch, flowers, and dividers.

We have to decide that we have a higher destination and that we can and will reach that destination when we live on purpose! Whatever race you have decided to run, you can finish!

To do that, one piece of our success will be to limit the external influences that we allow to help create our reality. We need to eliminate or drastically reduce the amount of influence that we allow from "Negative Nelly" or "Downer Don"!

Actuate

Once I create my vision for the year, I need to break down that vision into goals: benchmarks and checkpoints. These allow us to mark our progress along the way and give ourselves the psychological boost we need.

For me, it is much easier to run from checkpoint to checkpoint and let the overall race take care of itself.

"Good things come to those who wait"—but wait too long and your dreams will pass you by and be experienced by another man or woman of action!

Actuate means to "put into action," to "live it out."

All of us have things and/or pieces of our dreams that we don't know how to bring to pass—that's natural. If we could bring it to pass, completely on our own, it might be too small of a vision.

Success lies in taking the next known step: thinking in processes and asking yourself, "What would a successful person do in this situation? What is the next step they might take?"

Then take that next step, evaluate whether you are closer to your vision or farther away, and act accordingly.

The key is action!

> *"Don't be too timid and squeamish about your actions.*
> *All life is an experiment."*
> —Ralph Waldo Emerson

- Start what needs to be started
- Finish what I start

> *"Don't just be a hearer or thinker—be a doer—*
> *act on what you know to do!"*

All of this is great to dream and to act! However, maybe you need a little more process, a little more break-down to succeed. Me too!

So I asked myself, "*How am I going to do that?*"

Here are more thoughts with a deeper breakdown on keys and steps.

Elevate

From the words of my mouth, the thoughts in my mind and the meditations of my heart, I want and need to elevate my thoughts and my speech in order to elevate all areas in my life.

As I said earlier, we need to excise, or cut out, the negative influences in our lives. We need to control who gets to help shape and create the reality in our lives. No one can have input and effect in our lives unless we allow them.

Sometimes that is difficult. It may be a family member—it may be a boss—it may be a spouse! In these circumstances, we may not be able to change the proximity of the person (we may not be able to eliminate their presence), but we can eliminate their power.

This also comes into play when the negative, limiting voice comes from within.

Many times, the internal voice that reinforces all of the negativity is our own!

I fought more of that this week than in the previous six months.

This is where one of my early mentors used to say,

"We need to change our 'Stinkin Thinkin'!"

And this was a great little line (back in the '80s), but once again, my mind would say, "How?!" Then I heard John Maxwell say that the only way to erase a thought is to replace that thought. Trying not to think negatively is much like the exercise of trying not to think about Pink Elephants. The harder you try, the more persistent the thought!

If I was going to elevate my thoughts from negative to positive, then I would need to flood my mind with positive thoughts, possibility thinking, achievement-oriented, can-do thoughts!

Once my mind was full of positivity, my next conquest was my own mouth!

As a result of the many close influences to me, I had a real problem with talking about the negative expectations instead of the positive. At times, even now, I have to stop myself in midsentence and refuse to continue, because the thought was not going to be positive.

The loudest voice that resonates in our minds is our own!

I am extremely thankful for having a mentor this week that found a way to have his voice louder than my own. It renewed my belief in mentors and coaches.

From there, I had to determine to only let the positive come out of my mouth and to shut down the negative before giving them a voice.

Determine, with me, to speak only what is beneficial for ourselves and others!

And we come to another level of "How?"

Wait and Meditate

Spend time just being quiet, away from the hustle of the day. When I get up a few minutes early in the morning and spend the time reading a growth book—or thinking about all of the possibilities that the day can hold—it makes a tremendous difference.

During this time, I fill up with great thoughts from others and allow my mind to only dream about what can occur today.

Germinate

121

During this time, I expect the seeds of a great future to start to grow in my mind and heart—that I will experience a thought or thoughts that are going to be growing, stretching or solving.

Because I have this mind-set, I have learned to have a journal or writing pad with me. If I truly expect to have great thoughts during this time, then my point of action is to capture those thoughts for later action.

Percolate

Take time throughout the day or additional time in the morning to think more on the thoughts that I have captured. Again I have paper in hand, expecting that I am going to have creative thoughts that enhance and grow what I'm thinking about.

I determine to spend more time in purposeful thought around my immediate thoughts, my vision for the future, and, ultimately, my life by design.

Obligate

This is where the rubber meets the road. I have had this concept reinforced by most of my mentors: accountability yields results.

Most of us only achieve what others hold us accountable to achieve. Consequently, it is very important that we surround ourselves with positive people that care about our growth and share with them what we want to achieve in the coming year. The tough part comes next—asking them to hold us accountable and to serve as the race officials at each checkpoint or guides and mentors along the trail.

Give that person permission to call us on the carpet for not making progress toward the goals and dreams that we have set out for ourselves.

Select multiple people that may be a little bit further down the road in each of your desired growth areas; someone who is more physically fit, for your exercise goals; another who is better at relationships for your relational goals; and someone who is a little farther down the business success track for your professional development

Set a time each week when you touch base with each of these people to go over your progress. Maybe you could hold each other mutually accountable for the growth each of you desires!

One of the guys that does this tells the humorous, but true, story of working out three different times on Thursday just to be able to answer his accountability partner on their Friday call that he worked out three times this week!

So let's wrap it up:

For your year:
> Wait and Meditate, Germinate and Percolate—
> so that you can Create!

> Eliminate, Elevate, and Obligate—
> so that you can Actuate!

Together we can experience a better life run than the default that is bound to come our way.

Dream Big . . .
> **Engage in Possibility Thinking . . .**
> **Live and experience your Destiny!**

Meditate

*If everything in my life has been preparing me for this moment—
what's next?*

I closed my laptop, relaxed the muscles in my neck and let my head sink back against the headrest. I closed my eyes and just listened to the whir of the engines on the propjet. My mind's eye wandered back across the last week, the Alaskan terrain, and my team. I replayed many of the trails, the troubles, and the triumphs.

I must have drifted off to sleep and was awakened by a flight attendant asking me to put away the laptop, as we were landing for the plane change in Seattle.

Sitting in a coffee shop in Sea-Tac I looked at my watch, two more hours before the next flight. I ask the waitress for a refill of the coffee and looked out over the tarmac.

Inspiration started to hit. I always wanted to write a book but never felt like I could finish it. What could I say? How could I fill enough pages?

I decided to throw caution to the wind and fill my own prescription. There were a lot of unknowns . . . Would it be a traditional business book or an allegory? Would anyone read it?

It didn't matter. My first checkpoint was to get started and to get the thoughts out of my own head. I opened my laptop, took a sip of coffee and started typing:

Although the word Iditarod has several attributed meanings, I love two of them for our leadership discussion: One means distance or distant place and the other is said to mean "clear water."

Could there be a better tie-in to discuss the end game of leadership?

We need to achieve our goal, we have a distance to go, and in order to get there, we will need as much clarity as we can get our hands on.

Life and Business are adventures! Let's get mushing.
HIKE!

About the Author

Chris **Fuller** is an International Speaker, Author, and Consultant with experience in many aspects of business including Leadership development, sales, strategy, and finance. **Chris** has been developing businesses, motivating audiences, and training personnel for over 20 years. His passion for motivating others to "Dream Big" and to endeavor their greatest imagination is his cornerstone. Speaking to audiences of several . . . or several thousand, he communicates with natural enthusiasm. After he started his sales career early in life, it quickly became apparent that communicating was a gift.

Chris is President and CEO of Influence Leadership, Inc., a company focused on serving businesses and business leaders through the development and strategic growth of their people. Most notably, Chris is the world's leading facilitator and course developer of Dr. John C. Maxwell's content.

Chris has delivered keynotes and facilitated strategic sessions for an impressive list of companies, including key Fortune 500 clients like *State Farm Insurance*, *Pricewaterhouse Coopers*, and *Microsoft*. His experience in business and in working with such clients yields valuable, best-practice insights. Additionally, he has spent years pioneering and developing startup businesses and business units. His practical approach to achieving results has been replicated in dozens of ventures. The majority of his training and consulting has been done with not only executive level clientele, but has been strategically oriented toward middle and frontline management.

Chris received his Bachelors degree in Accounting from The University of Texas, Arlington. During his tenure, he earned many awards, including the Million Dollar Club with three different organizations. Chris resides in Arlington, Texas, with his wife Robin and four children. For leisure, Chris enjoys Scuba, skiing, fishing, music, and has participated in Sky diving, car and motorcycle racing, and, even, Alaskan Dog Mushing. Chris continues his work, aligned with non-profits, as a managing partner of an organization that aids families that have suffered from hurricane damage to their residences.

Influence Leadership

For more information on how to book
Chris Fuller or Iditarod Leadership,
contact Tawnya Austin at Just the Talent,
940.464.3653 or tawnya@justthetalent.com.

www.InfluenceLeadership.com
www.IditarodLeadership.com